READING BY
ALL MEANS

READING BY ALL MEANS

Reading Improvement Strategies for English Language Learners

New Edition

Fraida Dubin and Elite Olshtain

Addison-Wesley Publishing Company
Reading, Massachusetts • Menlo Park, California • New York
Don Mills, Ontario • Wokingham, England • Amsterdam
Bonn • Sydney • Singapore • Tokyo • Madrid • San Juan

A Publication of the World Language Division

Editorial: Kathleen Sands Boehmer
Production/Manufacturing: James W. Gibbons
Permissions: Merle Sciacca
Design: Dixie Clark/Beckwith-Clark, Inc.
Cover Design: Bonnie McGrath

Library of Congress Cataloging-in-Publication Data

Dubin, Fraida.
 Reading by all means: reading improvement strategies for English
language learners / Fraida Dubin and Elite Olshtain.—2nd ed.
  p. cm.
 ISBN 0-201-50352-2
 1. College readers. 2. Reading comprehension. 3. English
language—Textbooks for foreign speakers. I. Olshtain, Elite.
II. Title.
PE1122.D78 1990
428.6′4—dc20
89-32003

ISBN 0-201-50352-2
5 6 7 8 9 10–AL–95 94 93 92 91

Contents

Introduction

v

Thematic Organization

Introduction

TO THE USERS

This all-new edition of *Reading by all Means* keeps alive the strong elements of the first edition while introducing entirely new features in a textbook for people of other language backgrounds who want to improve their ability to read English, primarily for academic purposes. Not just an updated version, this all-new edition contains 27 selections. Of them, two have been retained from the earlier book—everyone's favorites; the other 25 readings are entirely new.

During the years that the first edition has enjoyed great success with ESOL students and their teachers, our audience has told us that along with interesting reading selections, engrossing activities, and a focus on strategies for successful reading, a new edition should also contain: attention to vocabulary building, discussion *and* writing activities, all in the context of thematically related readings. We listened to these suggestions very carefully. As a result, this new edition of *Reading by all Means* contains the best features of the first, plus much more.

The Design of the Book

The Units The five units each contain examples of a particular type of writing: personal narratives, introductory textbooks, feature stories, popular science, and non-fiction books, reviews, and profiles. Thus, users are introduced to a wide spectrum of writing styles. Further, each unit begins with an Introduction which points out some of the important characteristics of the writing in the selections, guiding students to adjust their reading to the particular material at hand. The unedited selections include writings by a number of outstanding authors.

With the goal of helping students become better readers in order to cope with academic work, we have followed the approach that to be a successful reader requires the ability to switch reading styles depending upon one's purpose for reading and the nature of the material. Limiting selections to purely academic sources not only ultimately defeats the purposes of mature reading, but also limits students' access to a broader range of information and knowledge.

Thematic Organization   The selections for reading are also organized thematically, (see page vii). By doing so, students are able to build their background knowledge about particular topics. At the beginning of a new reading, for example, they are reminded of what they have already read which will help them to understand the new material. In this way, the all-new edition has further developed one of the strong, innovative features of the first edition in which the idea of thematic reading was called "reading-in-depth." This feature puts into practice one of the important theoretical understandings of the reading process: the more one knows about a topic, the easier and more enjoyable it becomes to read further about it.

The themes which go across the five units have been chosen for their appeal to the academic interests of students at the post-secondary level. They include: Reaching out Across Cultures; The Role of Technology in Modern Life; The Business and Corporate World; Artificial Intelligence, Creativity, and the Human Brain; Theories of Evolution: How Did Man Evolve?; and Maintaining Life: Decisions and Dilemmas.

Internal Format   All the lessons are organized around a basic format, but with flexibility to make adjustments to different types of writing. Therefore, all of Unit Two and a few other selections that require close reading are highlighted with the title Guided Reading Activities. These activities stress careful reading of each paragraph.

Pre-reading activities include: A Note About the author, Before Reading sections titled To Think About, Vocabulary Preparation, and To Look For. These sections prepare students for the first reading of the selection. After the First Reading presents questions which stress understanding of the main ideas in the reading. Next come these words: "Now, read the selection again. Then go on to the section, Building Reading Skills."

The activities which occur after the second reading of the selection have been designed to facilitate students' understanding of both cognitive and rhetorical elements of the writing—the most advanced strategies for reading. The final section is Talking/Writing About, both small group discussion questions which grow out of the themes in the reading as well as a wide variety of individual assignments for writing.

Unit Two, which contains material from introductory college textbooks, guides students into close reading of each paragraph. Therefore, the organization is somewhat different since the aim is to understand details and facts, objectives tied to reading-to-learn, rather than reading-for-the-sake-of-reading.

Vocabulary   Reading unedited, authentic texts is a problematic assignment for intermediate and advanced ESOL students. On the one hand,
it works well for advancing reading skills. On the other hand, however,
it presents severe vocabulary requirements. As textbook authors for this
audience, we have grappled with this vexing question.

There are important features of this all-new edition which face the vocabulary load issue: 1) Vocabulary Preparation before the first reading
gives definitions for words which are key terms in the selection (words
and expressions which contain meanings essential for understanding
the main ideas in the passage). 2) Reinforcing Vocabulary activities appear in many selections after the second reading. 3) Personal Vocabulary-
Building Notebook, in which students keep a record of words they find
in their reading which they want to "make their own." (see section
below for details). 4) Context Clue activities guide students into using
clues in the context for guessing word meanings, when and if those
clues are actually there. 5) Students are advised to check on word meanings in their English-English dictionary at a number of crucial places. 6)
Students' attention is drawn to word and word groups which appear
across the selections, a consequence of utilizing thematically related
materials.

Strategies for Reading   A part of most ESOL teachers' repertoire today,
the idea of giving instruction in the ways in which good readers go
about getting meaning from a page of print was another innovation of
the first edition of *Reading by all Means*. Such strategies, however, cannot
be quantified or presented in some discrete list. In fact, organizing a
reading program around so-called strategies such as skimming, scanning, etc. probably discourages students from ever reaching the most
important goal of reading, namely to become caught up with the text
itself.

Rather, the approach in *Reading by all Means* has been to create lessons
which guide students into being able to understand good writers' words
and ideas. A key to the process is that each text is unique in itself.
Therefore, there is no fixed inventory of strategies. However, in many
ways the design of the lessons themselves incorporate strategies for
successful reading such as pre-reading, skimming for overall ideas, scanning back to find specific information, shifting one's reading style to fit
different types of material, etc.

In working with the texts in this all-new edition, we have paid close
attention to both cognitive and rhetorical elements through the pre and
post reading activities. For example: 1) summarizing the writer's main

point or message, locating main ideas, finding essential elements; 2) understanding details and examples, finding paragraphs which expand on main points; 3) using features such as the sequence of events, critical incidents, the time-frame, the organization of ideas; 4) reading across paragraphs, reading-in-chunks; 5) discovering implications and critical incidents; 6) making the material one's own through paraphrasing and summarizing.

A PLAN FOR TEACHING

Although mature reading is primarily an individual activity, the all-new *Reading by all Means* is designed to be used in preparatory and post-secondary reading programs as a classroom text. While it can be adapted to either individual tutorials or group work, ideally, a single lesson should be presented so that students have opportunities to read silently, complete many of the exercise materials by themselves, but then discuss their work and do the follow-up discussion questions with a partner or in a small group.

Presenting a Lesson

1. Students read Unit Introduction and A Note About silently.

2. Teacher leads brief discussion with the whole class which is centered on motivation for reading the selection.

3. Teacher introduces Before Reading: To Think About, To Look For, and Vocabulary Preparation should be carried out as class activities.

4. Students read the selection for the first time. Reading should be done silently.

5. Students answer After the First Reading questions. Checking answers with a partner works well at this point.

6. Note that Unit Two and a few other selections are not designed for two readings since the instructions for Guided Reading Activities take students into close, paragraph-by-paragraph reading of the text.

7. Students read instruction in text: "Now read the selection again, then go on to Building Reading Skills.

8. Building Reading Skills contains a wide variety of activity types. The teacher should be prepared to give directions for either individual, partners, or small group work. The activities, of course, are never meant to be used as tests of reading comprehension. Instead, they have been carefully designed, through analysis of each particular

text, to help students understand the rhetorical features of the writing, an important strategy for advanced reading of all kinds. Many activities also help students become engaged in the material in ways which foster cognitive development and strengthen higher-level thinking skills.

9. Talking/Writing About: In many instances, the discussion questions carry over themes from the reading passage into areas which involve students in looking at their own lives and experiences. In the writing assignments, students are encouraged to share their work with others through a first draft reading.

10. Teachers should select writing assignments carefully in terms of the level of their own students. Many of the ideas presented in this section could be elaborated on, modified, or re-structured to fit particular circumstances. By all means, teachers should feel free to do so.

11. Some General Suggestions: The units should be presented in the sequence in which they appear in the book since there are many instances in which the text refers to something which appeared in a previous selection, or in the accompanying activities.

12. The titles and instructions for activities vary from one selection to another in order to ensure that students read the instructions carefully rather than simply do the exercises mechanically.

13. Providing a pleasant and stimulating environment for reading is an important part of a reading program. Teachers are urged to do whatever is possible to augment the textbook with reading materials such as newspapers, newsmagazines, paperback books, etc.

14. At the suggestion of many teachers who found it limiting and unnecessary, this all-new edition of Reading by all Means does not contain an Answer Section. Teachers and students are urged to negotiate correct answers among themselves. If a case arises in which users are unable to come to agreement, or if they are unable to provide a solution, please contact the authors through the publisher.

Students' Vocabulary-Building Notebooks: Ultimately, growth in vocabulary learning is an individual pursuit. Moreover, students in most ESOL classes come with varying backgrounds and preparation for intermediate and advanced reading courses. Teachers, therefore, should encourage, model, and promote vocabulary-building as a vital, complementary activity to reading, but should emphasize that it is essentially up to each student to assume responsibility for his/her vocabulary-building work.

Throughout the lessons, there are ample activities which stress vocabulary. In addition, students are instructed to keep an individual **notebook** in which they keep a record of the words which they want to remember for future use. At the beginning of the course, time should be set aside to discuss keeping such a word-log.

Since vocabulary-building is really an on-going process—even in our native language we acquire new vocabulary throughout our lives—realistic goals should be set. For that reason, the vocabulary activities in *Reading by all Means* concentrate on word meanings as they are found in the selections. Even if there are multiple dictionary entries for a word, it is advisable for students to concentrate on the single meaning which fits the context of the passage.

A sample vocabulary listing for a notebook entry is shown below:

1. The word
2. The selection in which it occurred
3. The immediate context in which it occurred (the sentence or phrase)
4. Dictionary meaning which fits the particular context
5. Notes: (personal items of word association which might aid in remembering, recalling.)

ACKNOWLEDGMENTS ━━━━━━━━━━

Scores of teachers from many parts of the world have told us how much they enjoyed the first edition. We thank each one and hope this all-new *Reading by all Means* makes as many friends as did its predecessor.

We acknowledge with gratitude the suggestions and comments from our anonymous readers. In addition, we thank Ann K. Wennerstrom who did a careful and valuable reading of the first draft.

Our editor, Kathleen Sands-Boehmer, has extended understanding and support at every step.

The Authors

READING
PERSONAL
NARRATIVES

UNIT INTRODUCTION

READING NARRATIVES ━━━━━━━━━━━━━

From bedtime stories to myths, fables, novels, and serialized dramas on TV, the narrative is a universal form, used and understood by people everywhere. Yes, everyone likes a good story. For that reason, the all-new edition of *Reading by all Means* continues the pattern of the first edition by starting out with a unit on Reading Narratives.

In this Unit, you will read selections that exhibit a range of narrative writing types, from brief episodes which appear within the context of expository writing, as in the selections by Jacob Bronowski and J. Garrott Allen, to a full short-story by Paul Bowles. Along the way, you will also meet up with an old favorite, "The Green Banana," together with accounts by two other travelers, Paul Theroux, who starts off on a walking trip around England, and Jeremy Bernstein, who tells about the event in his life that made him decide to learn French.

The plan of the lessons guides you into strengthening your reading skills. Many important activities occur **Before Reading**. First, there is a preview of the material in the sections titled **A Note About, To Think About, Vocabulary Preparation,** and **To Look For.** Then, the instructions tell you to read the selection twice. The first reading is for getting an overall view of the main ideas. The second reading enables you to gain fuller understanding of the meaning.

The section following the second reading, **Building Reading Skills**, contains exercises which pinpoint features in the writing which fluent readers rely on for effective comprehension. The final section, **Talking/Writing About**, gives you an opportunity to expand on the ideas in the selection through group discussions and writing assignments.

Along with strengthening your reading skills, you will be adding to your vocabulary in English since reading and vocabulary enrichment go together quite naturally. In Unit One, you will begin keeping a **Personal Vocabulary–Building Notebook**, a record of words you discover in your reading of the selections that you want to remember and use again.

One important purpose for reading narratives should be for your own enjoyment. As your reading skills improve, you will discover the pleasure that comes from being caught up in a good story.

The Green Banana

A Note About . . .

In this new edition of *Reading by all Means* we have retained two selections from the first edition. "The Green Banana" is one of them because it has been everyone's favorite narrative. If you don't know what to do with a green banana, here's your chance to find out.

Have you ever eaten a banana that was not ripe? Was it green? Do you still remember the taste? An unripe banana should not be eaten, but it can be used for other purposes. In this short narrative, you will find out about other ways to use a green banana.

The author is concerned with cross-cultural studies—what happens when people from different nationalities and backgrounds come together. He tells what he learned while traveling in Brazil. He relates the story on two levels: he tells about his encounter (meeting) with the green banana; at the same time, he describes what he learned from the incident.

BEFORE READING

To Think About:

- What are the two lessons the writer draws from the experience?

To Look For:

1. What happened first?
2. Then, what happened?
3. What happened next?

Now, read the selection through without looking up unfamiliar words in the dictionary.

The Green Banana

by Donald Batchelder

1 1 Although it might have happened anywhere, my encounter with the
green banana started on a steep mountain road in the interior of Brazil.
My ancient jeep was straining up through spectacular countryside when
the radiator began to leak, ten miles from the nearest mechanic. The
5 over-heated engine forced me to stop at the next village, which consisted
of a small store and a scattering of houses. People gathered to look.
Three fine streams of hot water spouted from holes in the jacket of the
radiator. "That's easy to fix," a man said. He sent a boy running for
some green bananas. He patted me on the shoulder, asssuring me every-
10 thing would work out. "Green bananas," he smiled. Everyone agreed.

2   We exchanged pleasantries while I mulled over the ramifications of
the green banana. Asking questions would betray my ignorance, so I
remarked on the beauty of the terrain. Huge rock formations, like Sugar
Loaf in Rio, rose up all around us. "Do you see that tall one right over
15 there?" asked my benefactor, pointing to a particular tall, slender pinnacle of dark rock. "That rock marks the center of the world."

3   I looked to see if he were teasing me, but his face was serious. He
in turn inspected me carefully to be sure I grasped the significance of
his statement. The occasion demanded some show of recognition on my
20 part. "The center of the world?" I repeated, trying to convey interest if
not complete acceptance. He nodded. "The absolute center. Everyone
around here knows it."

4   At that moment the boy returned with my green bananas. The man
sliced one in half and pressed the cut end against the radiator jacket.
25 The banana melted into a glue against the hot metal, plugging the leaks
instantly. Everyone laughed at my astonishment. They refilled my radiator and gave me extra bananas to take along. An hour later, after one
more application of green banana, my radiator and I reached our destination. The local mechanic smiled, "Who taught you about the green
30 banana?" I named the village. "Did they show you the rock marking the
center of the world?" he asked. I assured him they had. "My grandfather
came from there," he said. "The exact center. Everyone around here has
always known about it."

5   As a product of American higher education, I had never paid the
35 slightest attention to the green banana, except to regard it as a fruit
whose time had not yet come. Suddenly on that mountain road, its time

4

and my need had converged. But as I reflected on it further, I realized that the green banana had been there all along. Its time reached back to the very origins of the banana. The people in that village had known about it for years. My own time had come in relation to it. This chance encounter showed me the special genius of those people, and the special potential of the green banana. I had been wondering for some time about those episodes of clarity which educators like to call "learning moments," and knew I had just experienced two of them at once.

The importance of the rock marking the center of the world took a while to filter through. I had initially doubted their claim, knowing for a fact that the center was located somewhere in New England. After all, my grandfather had come from there. But gradually I realized they had a valid belief, a universal concept, and I agreed with them. We tend to define the center as that special place where we are known, where we know others, where things mean much to us, and where we ourselves have both identity and meaning: family, school, town, and local region.

The lesson which gradually filtered through was the simple concept that every place has special meanings for the people in it; every place represents the center of the world. The number of such centers is incalculable, and no one student or traveler can experience all of them, but once a conscious breakthrough to a second center is made, a life-long perspective and collection can begin.

The cultures of the world are full of unexpected green bananas with special value and meaning. They have been there for ages, ripening slowly, perhaps waiting patiently for people to come along to encounter them. In fact, a green banana is waiting for all of us who leave our own centers of the world in order to experience other places.

AFTER THE FIRST READING _____

What do you think is the main point of "The Green Banana?" Select *one* from the list below:

- To tell about a clever method for repairing an automobile
- To point out that all people see the world through their own cultural beliefs
- To point out that people in so-called undeveloped places use very practical remedies

Now, read the selection again:
Watch for the paragraphs in which the narrative unfolds and those in which the writer comments on his experience. Ask yourself these questions as you read:

- What happened to the author on the mountain road in Brazil?
- Was the author a stranger in the village?
- Were the people there helpful to him?
- What did they suggest he do?
- Did their suggestion work?
- What did the mechanic say?
- Did the author agree with the mechanic?

BUILDING READING SKILLS _____

Finding the Sequence of Events

Below are the main scenes and the main events of the story, but their order is scrambled (mixed). Place the items in the correct order by writing numbers 1, 2, 3 . . . in the boxes.

1. *The scenes:*

   ☐ at the mechanics'

   ☐ on a steep mountain road in Brazil

   ☐ in a village consisting of a small store and a few houses

2. *The events:*

   ☐ the benefactor (villager) places a sliced banana on the radiator

   ☐ the writer seeks assistance in a small village

   ☐ the car radiator leaks

   ☐ the mechanic comments on green bananas and the center of the world

Finding Context Clues

You know that you can understand the meaning of new words by looking for context clues. Context clues can be words or phrases in the same sentence, the same paragraph, or anywhere else in the passage.

Example: If you do not understand the word *spouted* (line 7), you can guess its meaning from the words *hot water* which precede it, and the words *from holes* which follow. The meaning must be something like *to flow*.

In this exercise, use context clues to explain the meaning of the *italicized* words or expressions. Circle the correct meaning.

New words and expressions

1. Line 4: *the radiator began to leak*
   clue: the over-heated engine forced me to stop

2. Line 9: *he patted me on the shoulder*
   clue: assuring me everything would work out

3. Line 13: the beauty of the *terrain*
   clue: huge rock formations rose up around us

4. Line 15: asked my *benefactor*
   clue: "That's easy to fix." . . .
   He sent a boy for some green bananas.

5. Line 15: a tall, slender *pinnacle* of dark rock
   clue: . . . tall, slender . . . That rock

Guess the meaning

1. This means that the car:
   a) had mechanical trouble
   b) was out of gasoline
   c) was very old

2. This is a sign of:
   a) danger
   b) friendship
   c) anger

3. *Terrain* means:
   a) the village people
   b) the old car
   c) the geographical area

4. A *benefactor* is a person who:
   a) sells something
   b) helps one in trouble
   c) repairs cars

5. *Pinnacle* means:
   a) a high, pointed shape
   b) a large size
   c) a heavy piece

Discovering Implications

To imply means to suggest meaning without using words. A writer can imply information about the relationship between people, about people's attitudes, about events that might take place. As we read, we often add details that the writer only implies.

Line 6: This information is *given:*

> . . . the village consisted of a small store and a scattering of houses.

This information is *implied:*

> It is a rural village; the people are probably poor, without radio or TV; they see few strangers, have little education . . .

What information does the author of "The Green Banana" imply in the following? Discuss your answers with a partner.

1. Line 4: . . . the radiator began to leak ten miles from the nearest mechanic.

1. (Is the stranger afraid he will have car trouble?)

   _____*yes*_____

2. Line 10: "Green bananas," he smiled. Everyone agreed.

2. (Do the villagers know something he doesn't? What is it?)

   _____

3. Line 12: Asking questions would betray my ignorance. I remarked on the beauty of the terrain.

3. (Does the stranger feel awkward? Why?)

   _____

4. Line 17: I looked to see if he were teasing me, but his face was serious.

4. (Is the stranger suspicious? Why?)

   _____

5. Line 19: The occasion demanded some show of recognition on my part.

5. (Is the stranger trying to be polite? Why?)

   _____

6. Line 26: Everyone laughed at my astonishment.

6. (Were the villagers happy they could teach the stranger something? Why did they feel that way?)

   _____

7. Line 27: An hour later, after one more application of green banana, my radiator and I reached our destination.

7. (Was the green banana a successful solution? How did it solve the problem?)

   _____

8. Line 29: "Who taught you about the green banana?"

8. (Is the mechanic surprised that a stranger knows a local custom? Why should he be surprised?)

   _____

Discovering More Implications

Writers both give and imply information. What do we know about the people in the narrative? Some information is given; some is implied.

1. *The stranger:*
   a) given information:

      traveling in Brazil
      product of American higher education
      comes from New England

   b) implied information:

      speaks Portuguese
      travels a lot
      may be a writer

2. *The benefactor:*
   a) given information:

      _____

      _____

      _____

   b) implied information:

      _____

      _____

      _____

3. *The village people:*
   a) given information:

      _____

      _____

      _____

   b) implied information:

      _____

      _____

      _____

4. *The mechanic:*
   a)   given information:

   _____

   _____

   _____

   b)   implied information:

   _____

   _____

   _____

Summarizing the Message by Using Key Phrases

In line 42, the author mentions that he learned two lessons from his experience:

> "I had been wondering for some time about those episodes of clarity which educators like to call "learning moments" and knew I had just experienced two of them at once."

What are the two "learning moments" the author experienced? To help yourself express the two ideas, re-read the following key phrases in the selection. Then write a summary of the author's message in your own words.

1.   "Learning moment one": *Key Phrases*

   . . . the green banana
   . . . fruit whose time had not yet come.
   . . . its (the banana's) time and my need had converged (come together).

   "The people in that village had known about it for years. My own time had come in relation to it."

   Your summary: _____

   _____

   _____

   _____

2. "Learning moment two": *Key Phrases*

"I had initially doubted their claim, knowing for a fact that the center (of the earth) was located somewhere in New England.

Gradually, I realized they had a valid belief . . . and I agreed with them . . . every place has a special meaning for the people in it . . .

The number of such centers (of the earth) is incalculable (too large to be counted) . . ."

Your summary: _____

_____

_____

TALKING/WRITING ABOUT ━━━━━━━━━━━━━━━━━

Work with a partner or in a small group and discuss these issues. Remember, good listening is an important part of sharing ideas.

1. What information about the characters in the narrative is given, what is implied? (Share your answers to Discovering More Implications.)

2. What does the expression (line 36) "its time had come . . ." mean to you? Can you think of any person or idea "whose time has come"?

3. What is the special potential of the green banana? Is it useful? Is it symbolic?

Choose one topic from the list below to write about:

1. Do you agree there is a "universal concept" (line 49) about the center of the world? What is the center of your world?

2. What "learning moments" (line 43) have you experienced in your own life?

3. Have you experienced any cross-cultural learning moments? For example, in traveling, meeting new people, attending new schools?

Learning French

A Note About . . .

Jeremy Bernstein has had two distinguished careers in one lifetime. He is both a professor of physics and an author. In his writing, he has published articles and books about contemporary scientists in which he describes their work for non-scientist readers. He has also written articles about his hobby, mountain climbing.

BEFORE READING

To Think About:

1. This selection was taken from a larger context, Jeremy Bernstein's auto-biography, *Personal History*. It describes his experiences in college and during the period in his life when he was beginning his work in science. In 1959, with a new doctoral degree, he went to Paris on a fellowship.

2. While you read, think about your own experiences being in a foreign city, perhaps alone, not knowing the language very well.

To Look For:

1. There were two critical incidents that convinced the author to study French: What were they?

2. One of the incidents involved misunderstanding what a beautiful French girl said to him—in French. She used an unusual tense, simply to catch his attention. What was the result?

3. Learning French, both studying in a class and using it with French people, had an important result in Bernstein's life. What was it?

Vocabulary Preparation:

The article contains expressions in French. For example:

je vous aimais   I loved you / distant past

Some are the names of famous places in Paris:

Champs Elysées   a famous boulevard
Pantheon   a large church

Latin Quarter	student neighborhood
Sorbonne	university

others:

Michelin	a guidebook; gives "stars" to restaurants, etc.
au pair	a live-in baby-sitter; often a student's job

YOUR OWN PERSONAL VOCABULARY-BUILDING NOTEBOOK

As you read each of the selections in *Reading by all Means*, there will be words that are unfamiliar to you. *Don't* stop to look them up in a dictionary. Doing so will slow your reading speed, thus interfering with your understanding of the text. Instead, lightly circle unknown words with a pencil. After the first reading, select five or six words that you are the most curious about. Enter them in your Personal Vocabulary-Building Notebook. Your teacher will give you information about keeping it. In addition to your own word list, **Before Reading** will give you **Vocabulary Preparation** for some of the key words in each selection.

Learning French

by Jeremy Bernstein

1 [My plan had been to absorb French osmotically, from taxi-drivers, newspapers, my car radio, and waiters. This worked as long as all one wanted to do was to order a simple meal in a restaurant or take a taxi to the Champs Elysées. But it became clearer and clearer to me that getting beyond that stage was going to be impossible without help—a lot of help. It also became clear that unless I did, my year in Paris was going to be a lonely and frustrating one.

2 Two specific things occurred which convinced me that I had better do something. The first was a little reception given by the *commandant* of the Ecole Polytechnique for the faculty and visitors. I was invited to accompany Michel. It was evidently a very interesting and distinguished group of people. The tradition of mathematics at the Ecole Polytechnique had always been very strong. While I was there, the great mathematician Jacques Hadamard, who was in his nineties, gave some sort of retirement address. Laurent Schwartz, considered one of the greatest mathematicians in the world, was then on the faculty, and it would have been nice to talk to him and to the other people there. They were very polite, and were initially interested in the fact that I had come from America, but as soon as it became apparent that I could not carry on a sensible conversation in French their interest faded. I left the reception feeling like a moron.

3 The second experience was related to the fact that I had not managed to meet any girls. Paris in the fall can be one of the most romantic cities in the world, and it can also be one of the loneliest. Once the students got settled, the Latin Quarter burst into life. The cafes were full of flirtatious couples engaged in what I took to be scintillating conversation. The whole Latin Quarter, with its narrow side streets and curious buildings bathed in the soft light of autumn, was like one of those bittersweet French love songs.

4 One morning, I came to work early, by bus. By this time, I had decided that to keep my sanity I had better save my car for special occasions. Upon my request for a hint about driving in Paris, Michel had remarked, *"Mon cher,* if you want the right of way, take it." Instead, I began taking the bus. It was a lovely morning. I got off the bus at the station below the Pantheon. A beautiful red-haired girl was standing there. She made one's heart stop. Much to my astonishment, she ap-

proached me and said, *"Je vous aimais."* In my bewilderment and linguistic ineptitude, I did not notice that she had used the past tense. That dawned on me only later, after I had spent the equivalent of three dollars to buy the awful poetry magazine she was selling. That was it. I was going to learn to speak French.

5   At Michel's suggestion, I decided to go the Alliance Française, on the Boulevard Raspail, not far from the Sorbonne. It specialized in teaching French to foreigners; all the instruction was in French, and the only common language of most of the students was French. *"Très sérieux,"* Michel had said solemnly. The whole place had a no-nonsense sobriety about it. There were, as I recall, five levels, ranging from total novice to interpreter. The evening classes, which were what I was interested in, met five nights a week for something like two hours, and the cost was extremely reasonable. I decided to enroll in the second level, since by then I had a smattering of restaurant and taxi French. I was given a student card, which entitled me to eat in the terrible student restaurants in the Latin Quarter and probably legitimized my stay in the Maison de Cuba. There was the bonus that something like half of the class consisted of au pair girls from Germany, Great Britain, and Scandinavia.

6   The only other American in my class was another physicist, named Robert Tripp, who was a colleague of Ypsilantis's at Berkeley, and was also spending a year in Paris. I do not remember whether Tripp found his way to the class independently or whether we had discussed it in advance. In any event, we now engaged in fierce contests to see which of us could get the highest grade on the *dictée*, that diabolical examination in which the teacher reads a passage in French and one has to copy it down. Anyone who has done this knows the traps one can fall into with words that sound alike but have all sorts of different spellings and accents. Besides the *dictée*, we had homework assignments and regular tests.

7   In addition, there were hours and hours of classroom conversation, in which one got to know, to some extent, one's classmates. Many of them were refugees from Eastern Europe or Franco's Spain. Learning to speak and write French correctly was for them a vital necessity. Once a week, after class, Tripp and I treated ourselves to a late meal at one of the starred restaurants in the Michelin. Our ambition was to eat our way through the stars, and I still have the 1959 Michelin with the restaurants systematically crossed off.

8   In due course, I found myself with a German girlfriend from our class. She was in Paris as an au pair and had blue eyes that glowed like those of a porcelain cat. Life began to look a lot better.

9   Anyone who has really tried, especially in adulthood, to learn a

foreign language will probably never forget the moment when one discovers that one can think in that language. What critical mass of neural crossings must be achieved for this to happen I cannot imagine. It is a totally remarkable experience. It happened to me one morning a few months after I began my classes. I was driving somewhere with the car radio turned on, and it suddenly dawned on me that I was understanding the French directly, without making a translation in my head—a fantastic sensation. From that point on, I immersed myself in French. There were dozens of small night clubs in the Latin Quarter which featured singers like Jacques Brel and Ricet Barrier, both of whom were just becoming known . . .

10   Because I was living with students, my French was very demotic—student slang and worse. This had unexpected consequences a few years later, when I began climbing with the Chamonix guides in the French Alps. In my second year of climbing, I was assigned to Claude Jaccoux, who over the years has become one of my closest friends and about whom I have written a good deal. Jaccoux has told me that on our first climb, when he heard that his client was an American, his heart sank—the language barrier. He was astounded, therefore, to hear me emit at the first serious difficulty a stream of argot that would have done credit to a French sailor. He invited me to dinner with his family that very night, and from that all else followed.]

AFTER THE FIRST READING

- In the end, did Bernstein learn French by osmosis?
- What else did he do to learn French?
- What was the result?

Read the selection again. Then go on to the section, Building Reading Skills.

BUILDING READING SKILLS

Understanding the Critical Incidents

1. At the reception (para. 2):
    Bernstein left the reception feeling foolish ("like a moron") because he was unable to:
    a) discuss mathematics with the distinguished visitors
    b) find his way around Paris
    c) hold an intelligent conversation in French

2. (para. 4) The beautiful red-haired girl caught his attention by using an odd phrase in French. Actually, it didn't make sense, but Bernstein only realized it later. At that moment, he thought she had said:
   a) "I love you."
   b) "Please, sir, buy a magazine."
   c) "Can you help me?"

Context Clues

Some words and expressions can be guessed by using the clues in the immediate context. You should be able to understand the following:

guess the meaning	*clues*
1. para. 4 linguistic ineptitude _____	• bewilderment • I did not notice she used the past tense. • dawned on me later
2. para. 5 The place had a no-nonsense sobriety _____	• no-nonsense • *très seriéux* (French)
3. para. 10 My French was very demotic _____	• because I was living with students • student slang and worse
4. para. 10 . . . to hear me emit a stream of argot _____	• . . . would have done credit to a French sailor

Understanding the Details

Be prepared to talk over the answers to these questions with your partner or in a small group:

1. para. 3

   The writer felt sure the couples he watched in the cafes were having <u>scintillating</u> conversations.

Use an English-English dictionary to find the meaning of the underlined word, then write a brief explanation of the meaning of the sentence.

_____

_____

2. para. 4
"Upon my request for a hint about driving in Paris, Michel had re-marked, "*mon cher*, if you want the right of way, take it"

(note: Michel is French. He addresses Bernstein as, "my friend.") What did Bernstein do?

_____

_____

3. para. 5 at the Alliance Française (French language school):
"The only common language of most of the students was French."

What was the result? _____

_____

4. para. 7 Explain the meaning:
"Many of them were refugees . . ."

_____

_____

5. para. 9
How did Bernstein discover that he could "think in French?"

_____

_____

6. para. 9
What else did Bernstein do to become fluent in French?

_____

_____

TALKING/WRITING ABOUT _____

1. Brainstorm the writing assignment below in a small group. (Brainstorm means to talk freely, allowing the ideas about a topic to carry the conversation along.) When you have completed a first draft, share your ideas with the others for feedback (helpful comments), then re-write.

2. Write a personal narrative which describes a critical incident in your own life when you decided to learn English (or some other language).

You Have Left Your Lotus Pods on the Bus

A Note About . . .

Paul Bowles has gained a reputation as one of the most distinguished 20th century American writers. He has produced novels, several collections of poetry and short stories, and translations from the Arabic. He has lived outside of the United States for a great many years. Along with his reputation as a writer, he is also noted as a composer and ethnomusicologist.

BEFORE READING

To Think About:

1. This is a story about cross–cultural misunderstanding. When individuals from different backgrounds come together, they can easily misunderstand each other.

2. The title offers some clues about what to expect:
   - Do you think there will be a bus ride in the story?
   - Do you think there will be lotus flowers in the story?

To Look For:

In your first reading of the story, ask yourself:

- Where does the story take place?
- Who is telling the story?
- Who are the main characters?
- Which paragraphs are conversation? which description? which narrative?

Vocabulary Preparation:

lotus pods   the lotus is a flower of the lily family, often used as a motif in sculpture and architecture; a pod is the part of a plant where seeds grow.

Ceylon   the modern name is Sri Lanka

Siam   the modern name is Thailand

Words that appear in italics are not English, for example: *wat*

You Have Left Your Lotus Pods on the Bus

by Paul Bowles

1 I soon learned not to go near the windows or to draw aside the double curtains in order to look at the river below. The view was wide and lively, with factories and warehouses on the far side of the Chao Phraya, and strings of barges being towed up and down through the dirty water. The new wing of the hotel had been built in the shape of an upright slab, so that the room was high and had no trees to shade it from the poisonous onslaught of the afternoon sun. The end of the day, rather than bringing respite, intensified the heat, for then the entire river was made of sunlight. With the redness of dusk everything out there became melodramatic and forbidding, and still the oven heat from outside leaked through the windows.

2 Brooks, teaching at Chulalongkorn University, was required as a Fulbright Fellow to attend regular classes in Thai; as an adjunct to this he arranged to spend much of his leisure time with Thais. One day he brought along with him three young men wearing the bright orange-yellow robes of Buddhist monks. They filed into the hotel room in silence and stood in a row as they were presented to me, each one responding by joining his palms together, thumbs touching his chest.

3 As we talked, Yamyong, the eldest, in his late twenties, explained that he was an ordained monk, while the other two were novices. Brooks then asked Prasert and Vichai if they would be ordained soon, but the monk answered for them.

4 "I do not think they are expecting to be ordained," he said quietly, looking at the floor, as if it were a sore subject all too often discussed among them. He glanced up at me and went on talking. "Your room is beautiful. We are not accustomed to such luxury." His voice was flat; he was trying to conceal his disapproval. The three conferred briefly in undertones. "My friends say they have never seen such a luxurious room," he reported, watching me closely through his steel-rimmed spectacles to see my reaction. I failed to hear.

5 They put down their brown paper parasols and their reticules that bulged with books and fruit. Then they got themselves into position in a row along the couch among the cushions. For a while they were busy adjusting the folds of their robes around their shoulders and legs.

6   "They make their own clothes," volunteered Brooks. "All the monks do."

7   I spoke of Ceylon; there the monks bought the robes all cut and ready to sew together. Yamyong smiled appreciatively and said: "We use the same system here."

8   The air-conditioning roared at one end of the room and the noise of boat motors on the river seeped through the windows at the other. I looked at the three sitting in front of me. They were very calm and self-possessed, but they seemed lacking in physical health. I was aware of the facial bones beneath their skin. Was the impression of sallowness partly due to the shaved eyebrows and hair?

9   Yamyong was speaking. "We appreciate the opportunity to use English. For this reason we are liking to have foreign friends. English, American; it doesn't matter. We can understand." Prasert and Vichai nodded.

10   Time went on, and we sat there, extending but not altering the subject of conversation. Occasionally I looked around the room. Before they had come in, it had been only a hotel room whose curtains must be kept drawn. Their presence and their comments on it had managed to invest it with a vaguely disturbing quality; I felt that they considered it a great mistake on my part to have chosen such a place in which to stay.

11   "Look at his tattoo," said Brooks. "Show him."

12   Yamyong pulled back his robe a bit from the shoulder, and I saw the two indigo lines of finely written Thai characters. "That is for good health," he said, glancing up at me. His smile seemed odd, but then, his facial expression did not complement his words at any point.

13   "Don't the Buddhists disapprove of tattooing?" I said.

14   "Some people say it is backwardness." Again he smiled. "Words for good health are said to be superstition. This was done by my abbot when I was a boy studying in the *wat*. Perhaps he did not know it was a superstition."

15   We were about to go with them to visit the wat where they lived. I pulled a tie from the closet and stood before the mirror arranging it.

16   "Sir," Yamyong began. "Will you please explain something? What is the significance of the necktie?"

17   "The significance of the necktie?" I turned to face him. "You mean, why do men wear neckties?"

18   "No. I know that. The purpose is to look like a gentleman."

19   I laughed. Yamyong was not put off. "I have noticed that some men wear the two ends equal, and some wear the wide end longer than the narrow, or the narrow longer than the wide. And the neckties them-

selves, they are not all the same length, are they? Some even with both ends equal reach below the waist. What are the different meanings?

20   "There is no meaning," I said. "Absolutely none."

21   He looked to Brooks for confirmation, but Brooks was trying out his Thai on Prasert and Vichai, and so he was silent and thoughtful for a moment. "I believe you, of course," he said graciously. "But we all thought each way had a different significance attached."

22   As we went out of the hotel, the doorman bowed respectfully. Until now he had never given a sign that he was aware of my existence. The wearers of the yellow robe carry weight in Thailand.

23   A few Sundays later I agreed to go with Brooks and our friends to Ayudhaya. The idea of a Sunday outing is so repellent to me that deciding to take part in this one was to a certain extent a compulsive act. Ayudhaya lies less than fifty miles up the Chao Phraya from Bangkok. For historians and art collectors it is more than just a provincial town; it is a period and a style—having been the Thai capital for more than four centuries. Very likely it still would be, had the Burmese not laid it waste in the eighteenth century.

24   Brooks came early to fetch me. Downstairs in the street stood the three bhikkus with their book bags and parasols. They hailed a cab, and without any previous price arrangements (the ordinary citizen tries to fix a sum beforehand) we got in and drove for twenty minutes or a half-hour, until we got to a bus terminal on the northern outskirts of the city.

25   It was a nice, old-fashioned, open bus. Every part of it rattled, and the air from the rice fields blew across us as we pieced together our bits of synthetic conversation. Brooks, in high spirits, kept calling across to me: "Look! Water buffaloes!" As we went further away from Bangkok there were more of the beasts, and his cries became more frequent. Yamyong, sitting next to me, whispered: "Professor Brooks is fond of buffaloes?" I laughed and said I didn't think so.

26   "Then?"

27   I said that in America there were no buffaloes in the fields, and that was why Brooks was interested in seeing them. There were no temples in the landscape, either, I told him, and added, perhaps unwisely: "He looks at buffaloes. I look at temples." This struck Yamyong as hilarious, and he made allusions to it now and then all during the day.

28   The road stretched ahead, straight as a line in geometry, across the verdant, level land. Paralleling it on its eastern side was a fairly wide canal, here and there choked with patches of enormous pink lotuses. In places the flowers were gone and only the pods remained, thick green disks with the circular seeds embedded in their flesh. At the first stop the bhikkus got out. They came aboard again with mangosteens and

lotus pods and insisted on giving us large numbers of each. The huge seeds popped out of the fibrous lotus cakes as though from a punch-board; they tasted almost like green almonds. "Something new for you today, I think," Yamyong said with a satisfied air.

29   Ayudhaya was hot, dusty, spread-out, its surrounding terrain strewn with ruins that scarcely showed through the vegetation. At some distance from the town there began a wide boulevard sparingly lined with important-looking buildings. It continued for a way and then came to an end as abrupt as its beginning. Growing up out of the scrub, and built of small russet-colored bricks, the ruined temples looked still unfinished rather than damaged by time. Repairs, done in smeared cement, veined their facades.

30   The bus's last stop was still two or three miles from the center of Ayudhaya. We got down into the dust, and Brooks declared: "The first thing we must do is find food. They can't eat anything solid, you know, after midday."

31   "Not noon exactly," Yamyong said. "Maybe one o'clock or a little later."

32   "Even so, that doesn't leave much time," I told him. "It's quarter to twelve now."

33   But the bhikkus were not hungry. None of them had visited Ayudhaya before, and so they had compiled a list of things they most wanted to see. They spoke with a man who had a station wagon parked nearby, and we set off for a ruined *stupa* that lay some miles to the southwest. It had been built atop a high mound, which we climbed with some difficulty, so that Brooks could take pictures of us standing within a fissure in the decayed outer wall. The air stank of the bats that lived inside.

34   When we got back to the bus stop, the subject of food arose once again, but the excursion had put the bhikkus into such a state of excitement that they could not bear to allot time for anything but looking. We went to the museum. It was quiet; there were Khmer heads and documents inscribed in Pali. The day had begun to be painful. I told myself I had known beforehand that it would.

35   Then we went to a temple. I was impressed, not so much by the gigantic Buddha which all but filled the interior, as by the fact that not far from the entrance a man sat on the floor playing a *ranad* (pronounced *lanat*). Although I was familiar with the sound of it from listening to recordings of Siamese music, I had never before seen the instrument. There was a graduated series of wooden blocks strung together, the whole slung like a hammock over a boat-shaped resonating stand. The tones hurried after one another like drops of water falling very fast. After the painful heat outside, everything in the temple suddenly

seemed a symbol of the concept of coolness—the stone floor under my bare feet, the breeze that moved through the shadowy interior, the bamboo fortune sticks being rattled in their long box by those praying at the altar, and the succession of insubstantial, glassy sounds that came from the *ranad*. I thought: If only I could get something to eat, I wouldn't mind the heat so much.

36   We got into the center of Ayudhaya a little after three o'clock. It was hot and noisy; the bhikkus had no idea of where to look for a restaurant, and the prospect of asking did not appeal to them. The five of us walked aimlessly. I had come to the conclusion that neither Prasert nor Vichai understood spoken English, and I addressed myself earnestly to Yamyong. "We've got to eat." He stared at me with severity. "We are searching," he told me.

37   Eventually we found a Chinese restaurant on a corner of the principal street. There was a table full of boisterous Thais drinking *mekong* (categorized as whiskey, but with the taste of cheap rum) and another table occupied by an entire Chinese family. These people were doing some serious eating, their faces buried in their rice bowls. It cheered me to see them: I was faint, and had half expected to be told that there was no hot food available.

38   The large menu in English which was brought us must have been typed several decades ago and wiped with a damp rag once a week ever since. Under the heading SPECIALTIES were some dishes that caught my eye, and as I went through the list I began to laugh. Then I read it aloud to Brooks.

39   "FRIED SHARKS FINS AND BEAN SPROUT
CHICKEN CHINS STUFFED WITH SHRIMP
FRIED RICE BIRDS
SHRIMPS BALLS AND GREEN MARROW
PIGS LIGHTS WITH PICKLES
BRAKED RICE BIRD IN PORT WINE
FISH HEAD AND BEAN CURD"

Although it was natural for our friends not to join in the laughter, I felt that their silence was not merely failure to respond; it was heavy, positive.

40   A moment later three Pepsi-Cola bottles were brought and placed on the table. "What are you going to have?" Brooks asked Yamyong.

41   "Nothing, thank you," he said lightly. "This will be enough for us today."

42   "But this is terrible! You mean no one is going to eat *anything*?"

43   "You and your friend will eat your food," said Yamyong. (He might as well have said "fodder.") Then he, Prasert, and Vichai stood up, and

carrying their Pepsi-Cola bottles with them, went to sit at a table on the other side of the room. Now and then Yamyong smiled sternly across at us.

44   "I wish they'd stop watching us," Brooks said under his breath.

45   "They were the ones who kept putting it off," I reminded him. But I felt guilty, and I was annoyed at finding myself placed in the position of the self-indulgent unbeliever. It was almost as bad as eating in front of Moslems during Ramadan.

46   We finished our meal and set out immediately, following Yamyong's decision to visit a certain temple he wanted to see. The taxi drive led us through a region of thorny scrub. Here and there, in the shade of spreading flat-topped trees, were great round pits, full of dark water and crowded with buffaloes; only their wet snouts and horns were visible. Brooks was already crying: "Buffaloes! Hundreds of them!" He asked the taxi driver to stop so that he could photograph the animals.

47   "You will have buffaloes at the temple," said Yamyong. He was right; there was a muddy pit filled with them only a few hundred feet from the building. Brooks went and took his pictures while the bhikkus paid their routine visit to the shrine. I wandered into a courtyard where there was a long row of stone Buddhas. It is the custom of temple-goers to plaster little squares of gold leaf into the religious statues in the *wats*. When thousands of them have been stuck onto the same surface, tiny scraps of the gold come unstuck. Then they tremble in the breeze, and the figure shimmers with a small, vibrant life of its own. I stood in the courtyard watching this quivering along the arms and torsos of the Buddhas, and I was reminded of the motion of the bô-tree's leaves. When I mentioned it to Yamyong in the taxi, I think he failed to understand, for he replied: "The bô-tree is a very great tree for Buddhists."

48   Brooks sat beside me on the bus going back to Bangkok. We spoke only now and then. After so many hours of resisting the heat, it was relaxing to sit and feel the relatively cool air that blew in from the rice fields. The driver of the bus was not a believer in cause and effect. He passed trucks with oncoming traffic in full view. I felt better with my eyes shut, and I might even have dozed off, had there not been in the back of the bus a man, obviously not in control, who was intent on making as much noise as possible. He began to shout, scream, and howl almost as soon as we had left Ayudhaya, and he did this consistently throughout the journey. Brooks and I laughed about it, conjecturing whether he was crazy or only drunk. The aisle was too crowded for me to be able to see him from where I sat. Occasionally I glanced at the other passengers. It was as though they were entirely unaware of the commotion behind them. As we drew closer to the city, the screams became louder and almost constant.

49   "God, why don't they throw him off?" Brooks was beginning to be annoyed.

50   "They don't even hear him," I said bitterly. People who can tolerate noise inspire me with envy and rage. Finally I leaned over and said to Yamyong: "That poor man back there! It's incredible!"

51   "Yes," he said over his shoulder. "He's very busy." This set me thinking what a civilized and tolerant people they were, and I marvelled at the sophistication of the word "busy" to describe what was going on in the back of the bus.

52   Finally we were in a taxi driving across Bangkok. I would be dropped at my hotel and Brooks would take the three bhikkus on to their *wat*. In my head I was still hearing the heartrending cries. What had the repeated word patterns meant?

53   I had not been able to give an acceptable answer to Yamyong in his bewilderment about the significance of the necktie, but perhaps he could satisfy my curiosity here.

54   "That man in the back of the bus, you know?"

55   Yamyong nodded. "He was working very hard, poor fellow. Sunday is a bad day."

56   I disregarded the nonsense. "What was he saying?"

57   "Oh, he was saying: 'Go into second gear,' or 'We are coming to a bridge,' or 'Be careful, people in the road.' What he saw."

58   Since neither Brooks nor I appeared to have understood, he went on. "All the buses must have a driver's assistant. He watches the road and tells the driver how to drive. It is hard work because he must shout loud enough for the driver to hear him."

59   "But why doesn't he sit up front with the driver?"

60   "No, no. There must be one in front and one in the back. That way two men are responsible for the bus."

61   It was an unconvincing explanation for the grueling sounds we had heard, but to show him that I believed him I said: "Aha! I see."

62   The taxi drew up in front of the hotel and I got out. When I said good-by to Yamyong, he replied, I think with a shade of aggrievement: "Good-by. You have left your lotus pods on the bus."

AFTER THE FIRST READING

Now, read the story again. Watch closely for the changes in scenes as the story develops:

- Where does the story begin?
- When/where does the outing take place?
- What happens while they are seeing the sights in Ayudhaya?
- Where do they have lunch? What happens during lunch?
- What do they do after lunch?
- What takes place during the bus ride back to Bangkok?

BUILDING READING SKILLS

The Sequence of Events

1. Suppose you were asked to work on a film or video version of this story. You might begin the assignment by analyzing the sequence of events to find the major scenes. In the lines below, enter the paragraph number in which each scene begins. Give each one a title:

example:

paragraph	title
2	*the first meeting in the foreigner's hotel room*

Discuss your answers with a partner or in a small group. Suggest ways to the others to re-write their titles. Listen to their suggestions for your own re-writing.

2. Try arranging the scenes to make a three act play. What would be the titles of the three acts? Which scenes would appear in each one? Talk over your ideas with the others in your group. Be ready to listen to their suggestions, too.

The Author's Selective Eye

A short story appears to be like real life, but actually the author has strived to put in just the right details: the author has used an artist's selective eye. Below is a list of details that appeared in the story. In each case, is the element included (a) to give local color and enhance the mood, (b) to illustrate cross-cultural misunderstanding, or does it combine both? Discuss your answers with a partner or in a small group.

(a) details for local color to enhance the mood
(b) a critical element to show cross-cultural misunderstanding
(c) both (a) and (b)

1. _____ the foreigner's question about being ordained as a Buddhist monk (p. 3)

2. _____ the monk's appraisal of the foreigner's hotel room (p. 4)

3. _____ the monks' method of sewing their robes (p. 7)

4. _____ the foreigner's impression of the monks' physical appearance (p. 8)

5. _____ the tatoo on the Buddhist monk (pp. 11–14)

6. _____ the foreigner's necktie (pp. 15–20)

7. _____ the doorman's respectful bow (p. 22)

8. _____ Brooks' fascination with buffaloes (pp. 25–27)

9. _____ the foreigner's interest in temples (p. 27)

10. _____ the gift to the foreigner of lotus pods and mangosteens (a fruit) (p. 28)

11. _____ the monks' food restrictions (p. 30)

12. _____ the foreigner is overcome with heat and hunger (p. 35)

13. _____ the foreigner's interest in a Siamese musical instrument (p. 35)

14. _____ they all look for a restaurant (p. 36)

15. _____ reading the menu in English (pp. 38–39)

16. _____ only Brooks and the foreigner eat lunch (pp. 39–42)

17. _____ the foreigner's remark to Yamyong about bô-tree leaves (p. 47)

18. _____ the noisy person on the bus (pp. 48–61)

19. _____ Yamyong replied: "You have left your lotus pods on the bus." (p. 62)

YOUR PERSONAL VOCABULARY-BUILDING NOTEBOOK ———————————

In using an English-English dictionary, be sure to copy each word's meaning *only* with the definition which fits the context in which it occurs in the selection. Ask your teacher to check your work.

TALKING/WRITING ABOUT ———————————

Get ready to write by brainstorming with others in your group about your reactions to the story by Paul Bowles.

1. How does the author effectively capture the feelings of someone who is new or foreign to a particular culture?

2. What kind of distinctions does the author make between himself and people from other cultures?

3. What Asian cultures is Paul Bowles familiar with?

Next, listen to each other's ideas for stories. Then, write yours in the form of a mini short story:

4. Have you ever been in a situation where there was a cross-cultural misunderstanding? What happened? How did you feel? How was the misunderstanding resolved?

A Moral For Any Age

A Note About . . .

This brief narrative is just as timely and important today as it was when Jacob Bronowski wrote it. For that reason, it is one of two selections from the first edition of *Reading by all Means* which has been kept in this otherwise all new edition.

In it, Jacob Bronowski describes a real incident that took place in Los Alamos, New Mexico, the place where the first atomic weapon was developed. Professor Bronowski, who died in 1974, was a distinguished scientist, humanist, and optimist. He had faith in scientific thought and the human race. Professor Bronowski was the author of *The Ascent of Man* from which a famous television series was produced. "A Moral For Any Age" is an object lesson, a story that presents an example of right conduct. Through the telling of the story, Bronowski explains what morality means to him.

BEFORE READING ─────────────

To Think About:

1. Use your English-English dictionary to find the meaning of *moral*. You will see quite a few meanings listed. Copy the one you believe is the best for the meaning in the title of this selection.

2. A moral for any age is timeless. Why?

To Look For:

Read the entire selection even if you do not know all of the words. Do not stop to look up unfamiliar words. Ask yourself these questions as you read:

*   Which paragraph gives the background of the story?
*   Which paragraphs give details about the story?
*   Which paragraphs give Bronowski's purpose for telling the story?

A Moral For Any Age

by Jacob Bronowski

1 ₁ On May 12, 1946, Louis Alexander Slotin was carrying out an experiment in the laboratories at Los Alamos with seven other men. Slotin was good with his hands; he liked using his head; he was bright and a little daring—in short, he was like any other man anywhere who is happy in ₅ his work. At Los Alamos, Slotin, then aged thirty-five, was concerned with the assembly of pieces of plutonium, each of which alone is too small to be dangerous, and which will only sustain a chain reaction when they are put together. Atomic bombs are, in fact, detonated in this way, by suddenly bringing together several harmless pieces of plu- ₁₀ tonium so that they form a larger, explosive mass. Slotin himself had tested the assembly of the first experimental bomb which had been exploded in New Mexico in July, 1945.

2 Now, nearly a year later, Slotin was again doing an experiment of this kind. He was nudging toward one another, by tiny movements, ₁₅ several pieces of plutonium, in order to ensure that their total mass would be large enough to make a chain reaction; and he was doing it, as experts are tempted to do such things, with a screwdriver. The screwdriver slipped, the pieces of plutonium came a fraction too close together, and suddenly the instruments which everyone was watching registered ₂₀ a great upsurge of neutrons, which is the sign that a chain reaction has begun. The assembly was filling the room with radioactivity.

3 Slotin moved at once; he pulled the pieces of plutonium apart with his bare hands. This was virtually an act of suicide, for it exposed him to the largest dose of radioactivity. Then he calmly asked his seven co- ₂₅ workers to mark their precise positions at the time of the accident, in order that the degree of exposure of each one to the radioactivity could be fixed.

4 Having done this and alerted the medical service, Slotin apologized to his companions, and said what turned out to be exactly true: that he ₃₀ thought that he would die and that they would recover. Slotin had saved the lives of the seven men working with him by cutting to a minimum the time during which the assembly of plutonium was giving out neutrons and radioactive rays. He himself died of radiation sickness nine days later.

5 ₃₅ The setting for his act, the people involved, and the disaster are scientific: but this is not the reason why I tell Slotin's story. I tell it to show that morality—shall we call it heroism in this case?—has the same anatomy the world over. There are two things that make up morality. One is the sense that other people matter: the sense of common loyalty, of charity and tenderness, the sense of human love. The other is a clear judgment of what is at stake: a cold knowledge, without a trace of deception, of precisely what will happen to oneself and to others if one plays either the hero or the coward. This is the highest morality: to combine human love with an unflinching, a scientific judgment.

I tell the story of Louis Slotin for another reason also. He was an atomic physicist who made a different choice from mine. He was still working on bombs when he died, a year after World War II ended. I do not think the less of him because he took one view of a scientist's duty and I take another. For the essence of morality is not that we should all act alike. The essence of morality is that each of us should deeply search his own conscience—and should then act steadfastly as it tells him to do.

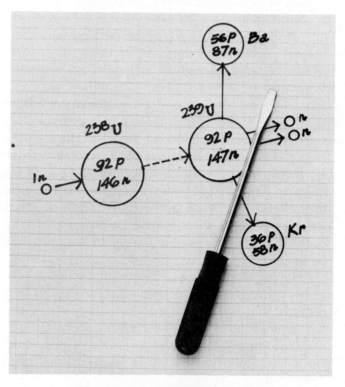

The formula for nuclear fission.

AFTER THE FIRST READING ━━━━━━━━━━

What do you think is the main point of "A Moral For Any Age?" Select *one* from the list below:

- To warn people about the dangers of atomic power
- To describe the heroism of Louis Slotin
- To make a statement about what morality means

Does the definition of *moral* you selected from the dictionary fit the context of the article?

Would you want to re-title the article?

Now, read the selection again.

BUILDING READING SKILLS ━━━━━━━━━━

Find the Organization

Scan the selection (go back and look for specific details in material you have already read = *to scan*). Look for the details in the three separate sections: background information (paragraph one), the accident (paragraphs two, three, four), and the author's statement about morality (paragraphs five, six).

Paragraph One: Background Information

- Who was Louis Slotin?

Paragraphs Two, Three, Four: The Accident

- What was he doing when the accident occurred?
- What caused the accident?
- How did he know the pieces of plutonium were too close together?
- Whose lives did he save?
- How did he save them?
- How accurately did he predict his own death?

Paragraphs Five, Six: The Author's Statement

- What two things, according to Bronowski, make up morality?
- What, according to Bronowski, is the essence of morality?

Discovering the Thread of the Story

Writers weave their words together as craftsmen do a rug or tapestry. One way to provide unity in writing is by repeating an idea or element. Look at these phrases.

line 2: . . . good with his hands . . .

line 17: . . . the screwdriver slipped (from his hand) . . .

line 23: . . . his bare hands . . .

What is the thread (the repeated element) that ties together these phrases?

Locating Details

Look at these sentences from paragraph one. In them, the author gives supporting details about plutonium. These facts are not the main point of the paragraph so they are set off by using a different tense. The events of the story are in past tense; the supporting details in present tense.

Fill in the blanks with verbs in the form in which they appear in the first paragraph:

1. Louis Alexander Slotin _____ _____ out an experiment.

2. Slotin _____ _____ with the assembly of plutonium.

3. Each piece _____ too small to be dangerous.

4. They will only _____ a chain reaction when they _____ put together.

5. Atomic bombs _____ _____ by _____ together several harmless pieces of plutonium.

6. The pieces _____ a larger, explosive mass.

7. Slotin himself _____ _____ the first experimental bomb

   which _____ _____ _____ in New Mexico.

8. What tense is used in sentence 7 in this exercise? _____

9. Why is it used? _____

10. What tense is used in sentences 3, 4, 5, and 6 in this exercise? _____

11. Why is it used? _____

12. What tense is used in sentence 1 in this exercise? _____

13. Why is it used? _____

Finding the Time Signals

Look at these sentences. In them, the author links what happened a year before the accident with what happened at the time of the accident. Fill in the blanks with the words and elements which signal time.

1. Slotin _____ test _____ the first experimental bomb which

    _____ _____ explod _____ in New Mexico in 1945.

    _____ , nearly _____ _____ _____ , Slotin

    _____ _____ do _____ an experiment of this

    kind. He _____ nudg _____ several pieces of plutonium together.

    The screwdriver slipp _____.

2. List the verb phrases in the paragraph above by tense form:
    past perfect:

    a) _____

    past simple:

    b) _____

    past progressive (*-ing* form):

    c) _____

Looking for the Asides

Sometimes writers put in sentences that are not part of the narrative. These comments, called *asides*, are similar to what happens when an actor on the stage speaks directly to the audience. The punctuation tells you that the phrase or sentence is an aside. It contains information that comments on the main idea of the paragraph.

1. In paragraph two: Find the aside in line 17. Write it on the line below. Make sure to copy the correct punctuation marks.

    _____

2. Choose one answer:
    In this aside, Bronowski is commenting on:
    a) Slotin
    b) Himself
    c) Experts

3. In paragraph five: Find the aside in line 37. Write it on the line below. Make sure to copy the correct punctuation marks.

    _____

4. Choose one answer:
   In this aside, Bronowski is commenting on:
   a) The disaster
   b) Morality
   c) Slotin's story

TALKING/WRITING ABOUT ─────────────

Work with a partner and discuss these questions. Listen and respond to your partner's replies.

1. What were Slotin's alternatives when the accident happened?

2. What would you have done in Slotin's position?

3. Have you ever made a very quick decision that affected others' lives?

With your partner, join another pair to form a small group. In your small group, talk about these issues. Then, select one to write about.

1. Do you believe the story about Slotin illustrates heroism, morality or both? Why?

2. Do you agree with Bronowski's definition of morality?

3. Do you know what a conscientious objector is? If not, look up the expression in the dictionary. Do you believe Bronowski approved of conscientious objectors? Have you had any experience with conscientious objectors? Share your ideas with the others in your group.

4. Do you believe everyone is a hero sometime in his/her life?

Neutron Weapons:

A Note About . . .

The author, J. Garrott Allen, is a retired professor of surgery at Stanford Medical School in California. He has written many scientific articles about the effects of radiation. This article, however, was written for a broad audience. Dr. Allen wanted people to know about the incident which he had witnessed in 1946.

BEFORE READING

To Think About:

1. Published in a newspaper as an opinion article about a news event in 1981, this selection is an eyewitness report of an accident that had occurred 35 years before. The event will be familiar to you since you have already read Jacob Bronowski's account of it in "A Moral for Any Age."

2. Remember that the author is a medical doctor. His narrative includes clinical terminology. Try to understand the main ideas without being concerned over technical terms. Or, check them in an English-English dictionary after the first reading.

To Look For:

- Where does the narrative begin?
- Where does it end?
- Does the author draw a medical or a moral conclusion?
- Where does the conclusion appear?

Vocabulary Preparation

Some key terms:

radiation the giving off of particles from an atomic nucleus
lethal dose a deadly amount
immoral not moral
(Note: find another meaning for *moral* in your English-English dictionary that fits this context)

Now, read the entire selection without using your dictionary.

Neutron Weapons:

by J. Garrott Allen

1   To minimize the horrendous devastation of nuclear warfare, exemplified by the bombing of Hiroshima and Nagasaki, the Reagan Administration has decided to produce the neutron warhead, which is designed to release enormous amounts of radiation while inflicting minimal damage to buildings and property in the targeted area. The principal advantage, we are told, is that the radiation would penetrate enemy tanks and rapidly kill military personnel, as well as anyone else within a radius of about 500 yards. There seems to be little awareness that many other people will receive lethal doses of radiation but will not die for weeks. months or even years. This poses medical problems of a magnitude never before considered.

2   Most physicians have not encountered patients heavily exposed to a sudden burst of ionizing radiation in which blast and heat are not components. I am one of the few who have.

3   During World War II, I was a physician on the Manhattan Project to build the first atomic bomb, and I witnessed the death of a 32-year-old physicist, Dr. Louis Slotin, who had been exposed to radiation during an accident at Los Alamos Scientific Laboratories in May, 1946. He was the leader of a group of eight men trying to join two pieces of nuclear material in order to create a critical mass. Slippage occurred that allowed a super-critical mass to develop momentarily, setting off an uncontrolled chain reaction and creating a sudden burst of ionizing radiation. Slotin had the presence of mind to immediately command the other seven persons in the room to remain stationary until he could draw circles around their shoes. He did this in order to identify their location so that later on their clinical courses could be correlated with the dosage of rems (roentgen equivalent, man—a unit of radiation) that each received.

4   In less than an hour, all were admitted to the local hospital: in that brief time, Slotin had turned a tragic accident into the nearest thing that we have to a controlled human experiment on acute total body exposure to ionizing radiation. Slotin had already made a rough estimate of his own probable exposure dose as being more than 1,500 rems, and on that basis concluded that there was no hope for his survival. From numerous previous experiments on dogs exposed to ionizing radiation, there was no doubt that, if his calculations were correct, so was his prognosis.

5   His clinical course resembled that of some of the radiation victims in the Hiroshima and Nagasaki bombings 10 months earlier who had been in locations where heat and blast did not reach them. Much of this radiation was

secondary, not direct, and resembled X-rays. Therefore, the exposure doses could not be nearly so well estimated. In the case of most of the fatalities, death was instantaneous from the heat and the blast, which extended beyond the bomb's radius of radiation.

6   The clinical results in Slotin's case duplicated what would happen to a person exposed to a nuclear tactical weapon, uncomplicated by the effects of blast and heat. During the first 12 hours, Slotin vomited several times and had diarrhea and a diminished output of urine. His hands, which had been the most heavily exposed to radiation, became swollen. Edema (swelling) and cyanosis (bluish discoloration) of the fingernail beds were noticed witin three hours of the accident. Also, patches of erythema (redness) appeared on his hands and forearms. In 24 hours, erythema was also noted on the chest and abdomen. By the following morning, massive blisters had formed on his hands and forearms.

7   After the first day, Slotin developed adynamic ileus (paralysis of intestinal activity), which could be relieved only by the use of a continuous suction tube through the nose. This tube soon became painfully irritating because of ulcerations that developed on his tongue and in the back of his mouth and nose. His hands and arms became increasingly swollen and painful. He required morphine for relief.

8   By the fifth day, diarrhea was frequent and uncontrollable. His hands had become gangrenous because the swelling had shut off the blood supply. The erythema and edema increased daily over his entire body. Frequent doses of morphine were the only treatment that was symptomatically effective. Nothing could be done to stop the steady progress of total disintegration of body functions.

9   On the ninth day, Louis Slotin died.

10   The autopsy findings were the same as those we had seen many times in experimental animals—hemorrhage throughout the body, the absence of platelets, and blood that would not clot.

11   The total body irradiation that this victim had received was later estimated at 1,930 rems. The other seven scientists in the room experienced much lower doses. The man standing immediately behind Slotin at the time of the accident, Dr. Alvin Graves, 34, received the second heaviest exposure, 390 rems. He eventually returned to work, directing many of the studies at the Nevada test site for several years before developing cataracts, becoming blind and dying at age 54 of other complications attributed by medical authorities in part to his radiation exposure in 1946. Two other members of Slotin's team subsequently died of acute leukemia.

12   There will be many survivors, both military and civilian, if and when nuclear tactical weapons are used. They will have received enough radiation to kill them, but for many death may be slow in coming. There is no effective medical treatment for serious radiation injury, and these deaths will be almost as agonizing to those looking on as to the victims themselves. The production of neutron weapons is probably as immoral a concept as human minds have yet devised.

AFTER THE FIRST READING ────────────

- What action by the Reagan administration is mentioned? Is the author in favor of this decision?
- Why is the author's experience unique? (in Paragraph 2)
- How does Allen's perspective on Slotin's accident differ from Bronowski's? Were both writing as witnesses of the event?

Read the article again and then turn to the section, Building Reading Skills.

BUILDING READING SKILLS ────────────

The Time-Frame

Paragraphs 3–11 include the narrative that is within the larger article. They tell the story of Dr. Louis Slotin. Which of these paragraphs (3–11) begin with expressions of time?

paragraph   *time expression*

_____   _____

_____   _____

_____   _____

Linking Ideas

Find the three time expressions that link together the sentences of paragraph 6.

_____

_____

_____

Summarizing Ideas

1. Look carefully at the verbs in paragraph 12. Underline them. They will help you decide if the paragraph is:

   _____ a summary of the   _____ part of the narrative
   writer's view   that begins in paragraph 3. How do
                                        the verbs signal this shift in time?

2. You were right. The author's main reason for writing the article is stated in paragraph 12, it is not part of the narrative. Find the sentence which best summarizes his overall point of view. Write it in the space below:

   _____

TALKING/WRITING ABOUT ————————————————

1. In a small group or with a partner:
   The title of this article is printed here just the way in which it appeared in a daily newspaper. Why do you believe there is a colon (:) after the words, "neutron weapons?" Suggest what should appear after the colon.

2. Have you ever been an eye-witness to an incident that involved danger? Do you know anyone who has been in that situation? Use your own experience or that of someone else to write a brief, factual narrative of the event.
   - What was the incident?
   - Who was present?
   - Why was it dangerous?
   - What actions took place? / What did people do?
   - How did you feel after the incident?

The Kingdom by the Sea: Getting Ready To Go

A Note About . . .

Paul Theroux has been called a first-class traveler and writer. He is a master at describing how things look, feel, taste, and smell in far-off places. But he also uses his talents to write novels and short stories. Essentially, he can tell a good story. After reading this brief passage from one of his travel-writings, you may want to read other books by him.

BEFORE READING ────────────────

To Think About:

1. "Where is the story?" "Where is the narrative?" These are questions that you will come to ask as you read. Actually, the selection is an example of how a masterful writer gets his audience ready for a story. Perhaps after reading this brief passage from *The Kingdom By The Sea*, you will want to read the entire book . . . or some other travel book.

2. What do you think about in order to get ready for a trip? The entire passage is an expansion of a few basic questions:
    *   Where should I go?
    *   Why?
    *   How should I travel there?

To Look For:

1. At the beginning (para. 1), a reader knows that Theroux's inner-debate about his trip had been going on for some time. The reader knows the discussion has been in progress. How does the reader sense this?

2. As you read, you will notice other indications of the writer's inner debate. Make notes for yourself: What are his arguments in favor of the trip? What are his arguments against the trip? What are the advantages (for him) / the disadvantages?

3. The writer's point of view: Theroux is an American who has lived in London for long periods of time. Look for the places in the passage where he refers to his identity as a foreigner (an "alien").

Now, read the entire passage without using your dictionary.

The Kingdom by the Sea: Getting Ready to Go

by Paul Theroux

1 [There were no blank spaces on the map of Great Britain, the best-known, most fastidiously mapped, and most widely trampled piece of geography on earth. No country was easier to travel in—the British invented public transport. And yet I had seen practically nothing of it. I felt ashamed and ignorant, but when I began to think about traveling around Britain, I became excited—because I knew so little. I wanted to write about it.

2 Writing about a country in its own language was a great advantage, because in other places one was always interpreting and simplifying. Translation created a muffled obliqueness—one was always seeing the country sideways. But language grew out of the landscape—English out of England—and it seemed logical that the country could be accurately portrayed only in its own language. So what was I waiting for?

3 The problem was one of perspective: How and where to go to get the best view of the place? It was also a problem in tone; after all, I was an alien.

4 The British had invented their own solution to travel-writing. They went to places like Gabon and Paraguay and joked about the discomforts, the natives, the weather, the food, the entertainments. It was necessary to be an outsider, which was why they had never written about Britain in this way. But it was a mystery to me why no one had ever come to Britain and written about its discomforts and natives and entertainments and unintelligible dialects. The British, who had devised a kind of envious mockery of other cultures, and who had virtually invented the concept of funny foreigners, had never regarded themselves as fair game for the travel-writer. They did not encourage aliens to observe them closely. They were like a tribe that plundered abroad and were secretive and inhospitable at home. The British did not make me think of Shakespeare but rather of head-hunters—their travel-writing a literary version of headshrinking that had never been used on them. I was eager to try.

5 But it was also a problem of itinerary. In a place that was crisscrossed with ant trails, a kingdom of bottlenecks and private property and high fences, my route was a problem, because there were too many routes.

43

To take all the trains would be no more than a mediocre stunt. The buses did not go to enough places. A bicycle was out—too dangerous, too difficult; another stunt. A car was too simple, and anyway I had lived in London long enough to know that driving on English roads was no fun. My route was crucial. It was the most important aspect of travel. In choosing a route, one was choosing a subject. But every mile of Britain had a road through it; there was a track across every field, a footpath in every acre of woods. Perhaps this was why I had never traveled in Britain: I had been unable to decide on the route.

6   And then I had my way: narrowly, around the entire coast. . . .

7   It answered every need. There was only one coast, it was one un- deviating route, and this way I would see the whole of Britain. In many respects, Britain *was* its coast—nowhere in Britain was more than sixty- five miles from the sea. Nearly the whole of the coast was unknown to me. And so as soon as I decided on this coastal route for my itinerary, I had my justification for the trip—the journey had the right shape; it had logic; it had a beginning and an end; and what better way was there to see an island than circumambulating its coast?

8   The greatest advantage in this tour was that a country tended to seep to its coast: it was concentrated there, deposited against its beaches like the tidewrack from the sea. People naturally gravitated to the coast, and they wore fewer clothes there—it was normal on the coast to be seminaked, exposed.

9   The best trains—the slow, sweet branch lines—plied the coast. Many of these branch lines were doomed. Some people said that none would be left in ten years, and most people agreed that the impending railway strike, planned for the early summer, would kill the branch lines. There were also the green buses—I had sometimes seen them filling a country lane, but I had never ridden on one. And there were footpaths.

10   I had an impression that there was a continuous footpath that went around the whole coastline of Great Britain. Every part of the coast I had seen so far had had such a footpath. Usually it was a muddy twelve- inch path, with a brisk figure approaching in plus fours and thick-soled shoes and a crackling plastic mackintosh, and carrying a bag of sand- wiches and an Ordnance Survey Map. I imagined this person to be just another feature of the British coast, like the old gun emplacements and the iron piers and the wooden groynes and the continuous and circling footpath. But if there was not a footpath around the kingdom, there was certainly a beach, and I could walk along the beach—from Fishguard to Aberystwyth, for example, where there was no connecting train. I would try to walk as much as possible; I would take trains if they were interesting lines or if the weather was bad; and if I had to, I would take

buses. It was so easy to speed through this country, I would have to make strict rules in order to slow myself down.

11   "England resembles a ship in its shape," Ralph Waldo Emerson wrote in *English Traits*. He was wrong: books by pious aliens were full of kindnesses of this sort. England, of course, resembles a pig with something on its back. Look at it. It is a hurrying pig; its snout is the southwest in Wales, and its reaching trotters are Cornwell, and its rump is East Anglia. The whole of Britain looks like a witch riding on a pig, and these contours—rump and snout and bonnet, and the scowling face of western Scotland—were my route.

12   No British journey could be original. Daniel Defoe had done the whole of Britain by road, William Daniell and Richard Ayton had sailed around it, William Cobbett had gone throughout the south of England on horseback, and more recently H. V. Morton and J. B. Priestley had gone in search of England, banging up and down in the thirties and forties. There were Britain-by-train books and Britain-by-bus books and books about cycling around. Some people had walked around Britain and written about it. The most impressive recent hike was that of a man who had walked every inch of the coastline. It was seven thousand miles, but he had been in a hurry. He had done it in ten months and practically walked his legs off—gave himself two severe pressure fractures in his leg bones. I had read his book. The trouble with travel stunts was that the trick was the thing; it was all a form of tightrope-walking, and the performer never took his eyes off his own feet.

13   I wanted to look around and see Britain for myself. I did not intend a stunt or a test of strength or a public display. In fact, quite the opposite; and later, tramping the coastal path or riding the slow trains, I sometimes felt like the prince in the old story, who, because he distrusts everything he has been told and everything he has read, disguises himself in old clothes and, with a bag slung over his back, hikes the muddy roads, talking to everyone and looking closely at things, to find out what his kingdom is really like.

14   And I wanted to see the future. Travel is so often an experiment with time. In third world countries I felt I had dropped into the past, and I had never accepted the notion of timelessness anywhere. Most countries had specific years. In Turkey it was always 1952, in Malaysia 1937, Afghanistan was 1910, and Bolivia 1949. It is twenty years ago in the Soviet Union, ten in Norway, five in France. It is always last year in Australia and next week in Japan. Britain and the United States were the present—but the present contains the future. A season of traveling with my eyes open in Great Britain, I thought, could not fail to show me what was to come. I was a little impatient with distant countries and past decades, but I was not necessarily looking for progress or invention. There was a deterioration and decay that seemed to me more futuristic than utopian cities of steel and glass.

15   And then an English friend of mine—just yapping—said, "The seaside belongs to everyone."

16   I knew this was exactly right and that I wanted to leave immediately.]

AFTER THE FIRST READING ────────────

- How do you know that Theroux is a foreigner? Where does he indicate his status as an outsider?
- There is a very brief mini story within the passage (para. 10). Why do you think the story of the old prince appeals to Theroux?
- Look at the outline map on page 45. Can you see the "hurrying pig" that the writer sees? (para. 11)

Now, read the selection again. Look more carefully for the paragraphs that reveal the writer's inner arguments in favor of/against the trip.

BUILDING READING SKILLS ────────────

Expanding Ideas

1. Much of the passage is an expansion of a basic question: "Why should I travel around England?"

   What advantages does Theroux find? List them:

   paragraph

   _____   _____

   _____   _____

   _____   _____

   _____   _____

2. For Theroux, the master-writer, the so-called disadvantages are issues connected with: "How should I travel?"

   What means of transportation does he consider? List them:

   paragraph

   _____   _____

   _____   _____

   _____   _____

3. What are the issues concerning the route?

   _____

   Trace the route he decides to take. Use the outline map on page 45.

4. Theroux also gets ready for a trip by doing his homework. He reads what other travel writers have written about his destination. What authors were on his reading list when he planned his walk around England? List them:

_____

_____

Enriching Your Vocabulary

Watch for useful words and word groups to add to your Personal Vocabulary-Building Notebook. In some cases the immediate context provides a clue to their meaning; in other cases, you must use an English-English dictionary. Which of the words listed below did you enter into your Notebook?

1. paragraph 2: *a muffled obliqueness*
   clue: "one was always seeing the country sideways"

2. paragraph 3: *perspective*
   clue: "How and where to go to get the best view of the place"

3. paragraph 4: *envious mockery*
   clue: the idea is in the entire paragraph "The British had invented their own solution to travel–writing . . . a kind of . . . of other cultures"

4. paragraph 5: *a mediocre stunt*
   There are no useful clues so use your dictionary; knowing *stunt* will help you understand the main idea in paragraph 9.

5. paragraph 11: *pious aliens*
   clue: "R. W. Emerson wrote . . ."
   Emerson was an American author, but you will need to look up *pious*.

TALKING/WRITING ABOUT ————————

1. In a small group, consider the provocative statement Theroux makes in paragraph 14:
   Theroux has traveled in many parts of the world. He sees countries in terms of specific time-periods in history. Do you agree with his time designations? Do you believe there are "timeless" places on the earth?

2. Use Theroux' writing as an inspiration for your own by writing about:
   * a trip you are thinking of taking
   or
   * a trip you have already taken
   Try to ask a basic question. Then, expand on the answer in two or three pages of writing.

READING
INTRODUCTORY
TEXTBOKS

READING INTRODUCTORY TEXTBOOKS FOR BASIC INFORMATION

The readings in Unit Two are taken from textbooks used in introductory courses in secondary, preparatory, and college curricula. Because these selections were written to teach subject content, they are quite different from those you read in Unit One. For that reason, your approach to reading must shift. Now, the objective is to read-to-learn.

In each case, these readings were taken from larger writings—an entire textbook. So at times you will come across references to other parts of the book. As you read, remember that textbook authors present summaries of others' ideas. They try to organize entire fields of knowledge in order to give students a broad overview of the field. Sometimes a group of authors contributes separate chapters to a book, as in the final selection in Unit Two.

Since the material differs from the narratives in Unit One, your strategies for reading should shift as well. Now it is important to:

remember facts, or use short-term learning, understand concepts, or activate cognitive learning.

Accordingly, the activities in Unit Two have changed, too. The section called **Guided Reading Activities** enables you to focus on close reading of paragraphs and groups of paragraphs, an effective learning technique. In **Building Reading Skills** there are exercises for using the information acquired through reading in other forms: filling in charts and graphs, completing information, etc. At the same time, you will discover that reading-to-learn is enhanced through **Talking and Writing About** the ideas you have discovered through reading.

The basic information you acquire in Unit Two while reading-to-learn will be utilized again when you read about some of the same topics, though from quite different perspectives, in Units Three, Four, and Five. Check the listing of Thematic Organization on page vii to see what other selections are related to those in Unit Two.

Intercultural Communication: A Voyage of Discovery

BEFORE READING

To Think About:

1. The title, "A Voyage of Discovery," could mean any of the following ideas. Discuss the meaning of each:

   a) taking a trip to a place unknown to you personally

   b) looking for places unknown to the rest of the world

   c) taking time to look into your own personal view of life in order to "discover" who you are

   d) going into a new field or area or interest in order to learn something new

2. Read the subtitles: Then, answer a) and b):

   a) The subtitle of 8.1 is "Intercultural Encounters of the Disturbing Kind." What do you expect this section to deal with? To help you guess what the section is all about, the author includes a statement which is broken up in three different parts:

   "Learning a new culture can be embarrassing . . . maddening . . . and confusing."

   Do you believe this section presents examples of "unpleasant encounters with another culture?"

   b) The subtitle for 8.2 is "Coming to Terms." This expression means "to reach a point of understanding and agreement with something which has created a conflict." If the first section deals with examples of difficult encounters, do you believe this section deals with ways in which we learn to overcome such difficulties?

Vocabulary Preparation

Some key words in this selection are:

culture	behavior which is typical of an entire community
cross-culture	between or across two or more cultures
culture learning	learning to understand a culture
intercultural communication	communication between cultures

Skim the whole passage. (To skim is to read as quickly as possible, just looking for main ideas.) It consists of a brief introduction followed by sections 8.1 and 8.2.

Now, use the Guided Reading Activities as you read the selection again.

GUIDED READING ACTIVITIES ────────────

1. In the first paragraph: The following non-positive words are used: unfamiliar, unknown, uncharted, incomprehensible, inevitable. (If you are not sure of the meaning of any one of these words, look it up in an English-English dictionary. Remember, grammatically, *un-* means "not.")

2. What are some of the non-positive terms used in the second paragraph?

    _____

    Whose feelings do these words describe?

3. In paragraphs 1 and 2: which of the following are solutions suggested by the author?
    a) we should consider unpleasant encounters with the unknown as useful experiences in learning about another culture
    b) we should learn more about intercultural contact
    c) we should avoid intercultural contact as much as possible
    d) we should try to keep our own culture and thus not have to undergo change and frustration

4. In section 8.1: As you probably expected from your prediction about the passage before reading it, this section contains at least three examples of intercultural contact which were not successful.
    a) Why was the first embarrassing?
    b) Why was the second maddening?
    c) Why was the third confusing?

5. Find the main ideas in section 8.1. Give examples from your own culture which illustrate these main ideas. Discuss your own examples and listen to others'.

6. Paragraph 8 contains words which you may want to look up in an English-English dictionary. Its function is to prepare readers for the main ideas in section 8.2. What do you think the objective of section 8.2 will be?

    What words in paragraph 8 are possible entries for your Personal Vocabulary-Building Notebook?

7. In section 8.2: The key sentence in paragraph 9 is: "This state of affairs is not necessarily detrimental; it does force the student of the field to accept various points of view and avoid a one-dimensional approach to basic concepts."

Intercultural Communication: A Voyage of Discovery

by Louise Damen

1 Moving about in an unfamiliar environment, at home or abroad, is often not unlike a voyage into the unknown, the uncharted, and, alas, the incomprehensible. Yet these inevitable sallies into the new and unfamiliar that mark all our lives can become less fearsome if they are simply regarded as exercises in culture learning.

2   One might well ask why the meeting of the new and strange so often brings embarrassment, confusion, or even anger. Why do so many visitors, sojourners, and immigrants feel as though they have become invisible in a strange country or, if not invisible, adrift without any sense of personal or cultural identity? The answers to these questions lie in the processes of cultural change and acculturation; they also lie in the examination of these processes at work in episodes of intercultural contact.

8.1 INTERCULTURAL ENCOUNTERS OF THE DISTURBING KIND

Learning a new culture can be embarrassing . . .

3   The grateful Latin American student, hoping to express his appreciation to his teacher for her efforts to improve his English, chose to send her the card on page 54. After all, she was so *simpatica*!

. . . maddening

4   The Japanese hosts to a group of North American teacher/students arranged for their guests to be housed in pairs in the student dormitory on the campus of the university they were visiting in Japan. After all, reasoned the hosts, it would be frightening to be alone in a foreign country. Yet these honored guests soon staked out their own ranges and settled down, one to a room, in red, white, and blue solitude. These inscrutable *gaijin*!

. . . and confusing.

5   Abdul Aziz never came to class on Friday afternoon. As a result, he often missed tests, which were scheduled for the end of the week. When his teacher pointed out that the seeds of failure lay in these

absences, he shrugged his shoulders and muttered, *"Inshallah."* "I understand that you must pray, but," countered the teacher, "you are in a foreign country and you may be excused from these responsibilities." After all, she concluded, first things first.

6   These vignettes of cross-cultural encounters illustrate not only the perils of unwarranted cultural assumptions as to what is translatable, what is frightening and what is not, and where priorities lie, but also the pain of learning the hard way.

7   Culture learning, or understanding the new ways of another group (or even one's own), is very like looking into a shadowed mirror. The broad lines of the reflected images are clear enough, but the muted light obscures details and forces viewers to fill in the gaps from their own experiences and cultural assumptions.

8   One means to cast some light on the nature of culture learning and cultural investigation is to review some of the methods and techniques that have been employed by professional cross-cultural researchers in the past. Valuable insights can be gained by assessing the hazards involved in such research and the solutions proposed. First, however, we must come to terms with some important concepts.

8.2 COMING TO TERMS

9 The field of intercultural communication has been a debtor in its exchanges with other social sciences; not only methods of analysis but also terminology have been freely borrowed. Because basic terms, such as *perception, acculturation, enculturation,* and even *culture* itself, have been defined in different ways in these disciplines, the unwary may find themselves confused by the variety of terms and seemingly contradictory definitions. This state of affairs is not necessarily detrimental; it does force the student of the field to accept various points of view and avoid a one-dimensional approach to basic concepts.

10 Before proceeding to a discussion of the nature of culture learning, several fundamental concepts, already introduced, need a more formal introduction. These include:

> *acculturation / enculturation*
> *cross-cultural awareness*
> *cultural identity*
> *cultural patterns, themes, and postulates*

11 Each of these definitions will be further refined and exemplified in ensuing discussions of the methods of cultural analysis and culture teaching. Additional definitions are included in the Glossary.

Acculturation/Enculturation

12 Culture learning is a natural process in which human beings internalize the knowledge needed to function in a societal group. It may occur in the native context as *enculturation* or in a non-native or secondary context as *acculturation*. Fundamentally, learning a first culture is a process of indoctrination. Enculturation builds a sense of cultural or social identity, a network of values and beliefs, patterned ways of living, and, for the most part, ethnocentrism, or belief in the power and the rightness of native ways. Acculturation, on the other hand, involves the process of pulling out the world view or *ethos* of the first culture, learning new ways of meeting old problems, and shedding ethnocentric evaluations.

Cross-cultural Awareness

13 Cross-cultural awareness involves uncovering and understanding one's own culturally conditioned behavior and thinking, as well as the patterns of others. Thus, the process involves not only perceiving the similarities and differences in other cultures but also recognizing the givens of the native culture or, as Hall says, our own "hidden culture" (1969).

14   Hanvey (1979:53) describes several levels of cross-cultural informational awareness: (1) awareness of superficial or very visible cultural traits (stereotyping); (2) awareness of significant and subtle highly contrastive traits; and (3) awareness of an insider's point of view of a given culture.

15   Cross-cultural awareness is the force that moves a culture learner across the acculturation continuum from a state of no understanding of, or even hostility to, a new culture to near total understanding; from monoculturalism to bi- or multiculturalism. Of course, the polar states are seldom observed. One cannot live very long and remain totally monocultural in the modern world. On the other hand, achieving a full state of acculturation is equally difficult. The facilitation of the journey along this acculturation continuum is of primary concern to the teacher. The final destination is a matter for the learner to decide.

Cultural Identity

16   Cultural identity refers to the relationship between the individual and society. Lum (1982:386) writes that "identity cannot be found by drawing apart from society. Identity is a social process in which one balances what s/he thinks oneself to be and what others believe that one to be. . . ." It is the cultural or social identity that is at stake when the process of acculturation is under way. To become bicultural is to develop an altered cultural personality and identity.

Cultural Patterns, Themes, and Postulates

17   The term cultural patterns, as used in anthropological and sociological literature, describes the systematic and often repetitive nature of human behavior, interaction, and organization. This is to say that human behavior is channeled and constrained by underlying systems that impose regularity and rules on which otherwise might be random activity. These systems permit the development of "patterns" of customary or expected behavior. The linguistic analogy is helpful here. Just as language users must recognize and obey the rules, conventions, norms, and system of the language they speak if they are to communicate with other speakers of that language, so must culture bearers recognize and be constrained, albeit in lesser degree, by the regularities or customs of the cultures in which they function.

18   This means that cultural behavior is more ordered than might appear from superficial observation; it is affected by the presence of customary or normative patterns. These patterns represent expected or acceptable

behavior in given cultures. The anthropologist studying a specific group will not only observe individual and idiosyncratic behavior but will also observe modal or expected behavior. A member of a given group when queried concerning a specific modal pattern is likely to answer, "That's the way we do it," or "That's our custom." For example, behaviors related to family relationships in any culture are not simply random, but will follow in some degree the expected and customary norms. The constellation of the behaviors and norms surrounding the family relationship constitutes a different pattern in Culture *A* than it does in Culture *B*. Thus, although we all take nourishment, there are culture-specific rules concerning what to eat, when, on what kinds of tables, and even for what purposes. Caterpillars, anyone?

BUILDING READING SKILLS ⎯⎯⎯⎯⎯⎯⎯⎯

1. In 8.2: Which of the following expressions belong to a one-dimensional approach and which to a multi-dimensional approach? Put the following words and expressions in the proper column: a narrow view; a limited perspective; an open minded approach; an only way of doing things; alternative ways for doing things; considering various approaches to the same problem.

    One-Dimensional   *Multi-Dimensional*

2. Give your own simplified definition of the following words and expressions based on your reading of section 8.2:
    a) acculturation
    b) enculturation
    c) cross-cultural awareness
    d) cultural identity
    e) normative behavior

3. Give examples of some normative or typical patterns of behavior in your own culture.

4. Draw a branching diagram of the way in which the ideas are presented in this selection by filling in the blanks below:

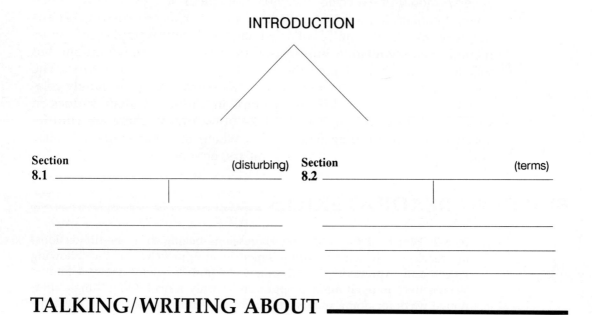

INTRODUCTION

Section 8.1 _____ (disturbing) **Section 8.2** _____ (terms)

TALKING/WRITING ABOUT ━━━━━━━━

1. Give some examples of intercultural misunderstandings based on your reading of the selections in Unit One. Scan "The Green Banana" and "You Left Your Lotus Pods on the Bus" for examples.

2. Write about an example of a cultural misunderstanding in your own life. Use the narrative form: what happened first; then what happened; how did the event conclude? What did you learn from the event?

Biology: Evolution

BEFORE READING ━━━━━━━━━━━━━━━━━━━

To Think About:

1. What do you already know about Charles Darwin?
2. What do you already know about the theory of evolution?

Now, use the Guided Reading Activities as you read the selection.

GUIDED READING ACTIVITIES ━━━━━━━━━

1. In the Introduction: Notice that there are five paragraphs. What words begin each paragraph? What is the main idea in each paragraph?

	first word	*main idea*
p. 1	_____	_____
p. 2	_____	_____
p. 3	_____	_____
p. 4	_____	_____
p. 5	_____	_____

2. What are the three main theories developed by Darwin that have had such an impact on the western world?

    a) _____

    b) _____

    c) _____

3. In 'The Origin of Species,' the last sentence of paragraph 6 presents a summary of the whole paragraph. It states that a theory of evolution must tell us two things:

    a) how organisms _____

    b) how _____

4. Look for the definition of speciation in 'What is a Species?'. Check your understanding of it by giving your own definition:

_____

5. Find the main idea in each of the four paragraphs in 'What is a Species?'

p. 7 _____

p. 8 _____

p. 9 _____

p. 10 _____

6. In the Summary: Define these terms:

a) natural selection is _____

_____

b) a gene pool is _____

_____

7. Be prepared to explain the process of speciation in your own words to a partner or in a small group.

Biology: Evolution

by John W. Kimball

Introduction

1 In 1859, the British naturalist Charles Darwin published *The Origin of Species*. It has been claimed that this book ranks second only to the Holy Bible in its impact on the thinking of the western world. What did it say that made it so influential?

2 First, *The Origin of Species* said that all living things on earth are here as a result of descent, with modification, from a common ancestor. This is the theory of **evolution**. Expressed another way, it tells us that species are not fixed, unchanging things but have, on the contrary, evolved through a process of gradual change from pre-existing, different species. The theory implies, too, that all species are cousins, that is, any two species on earth have shared a common ancestor at some point in their history. This theory of evolution directly contradicts the still widely accepted idea that species are unchangeable, each species having been placed on earth in its present form.

3 Second, Darwin's *The Origin of Species* presented a large number of facts that Darwin felt could best be explained by a theory of evolution and could not be adequately explained by a theory of special creation. In this chapter, we shall examine some of these facts along with additional evidence that has been discovered since Darwin's time.

4 Finally, Darwin proposed a mechanism to explain how evolutionary change takes place. This theory, the theory of **natural selection**, is the cornerstone of *The Origin of Species*. The idea of evolutionary change is very old. Evidence to support it had been presented before Darwin's time. It was Darwin, however, who built an overwhelmingly impressive case for the existence of evolution *and* proposed a theory to explain how evolution works. This theory and its clarification and enlargement by later workers will be discussed in the next chapter.

5 The idea of evolution provides a plausible explanation for a host of otherwise hard-to-explain facts. Let us now turn our attention to these.

• • •

THE ORIGIN OF SPECIES

6 The idea of evolution involves two processes. First is the gradual change in genotype and phenotype of a population of living organisms. Usually these changes are adaptive; that is, the organisms become increasingly efficient at exploiting their environment. Second is the formation of new species. If we assume that life has arisen only once on the earth, the 1.2 million known species of microorganisms, plants, and animals living today (not to mention all the species that have

become extinct) must have arisen from ancestors that they shared in common. So a theory of evolution must tell us not only how organisms become better adapted to their environment but also how *new* species are produced.

What is a Species?

7 The zoologist Ernst Mayr defines a species as an actually or potentially interbreeding natural population which does not interbreed with other such populations even when there is opportunity to do so. We must qualify this somewhat by adding that if on rare occasions breeding between species does take place, the offspring produced are not so fertile and/or efficient as either of their parents. Although a horse and donkey can breed together, the mule resulting is sterile. (In plants, even this restriction sometimes fails to apply if conditions in the habitat have altered. Plant hybrids *may* be more successful than either parent in such areas.)

8   It seems quite clear that the process of evolutionary change in a population and the process of species formation are related. Over a period of time, the accumulation of changes in the gene pool of a population must reach a point where we may say that a new species has been formed. This involves a purely arbitrary judgment, however. Who is to say just when the transition was made from one species to the next? Even if we could resurrect some of the ancestral forms to see if they could breed successfully with their modern descendants, our question would remain unanswered. An unbro-

ken line of forms stretches back in time from each living species, and the breaking up of this line into distinct species is an entirely arbitrary (although useful) operation.

9   Evolution has not, however, been just a matter of gradual change in a *single* genealogical line. The fossil record tells us that there has been a marked expansion in the number of species present on the earth. To put this another way, we believe that all our present species have diverged from common ancestors and initially from a single, first form of life. What can the theory of evolution tell us about **speciation**, that is, the formation of many species from few?

10 Speciation, as we have described it, is a gradual process. It begins with differences between individuals in a population, proceeds to the accumulation of consistent differences found at the subspecies level, and ends with the fixed differences associated with species formation. The entire procedure may take hundreds or thousands of years to be completed.

Summary

11 Evolutionary change in a species depends on (1) the existence of genetic variability among the individuals in the species, which leads to (2) differential reproductive success among them. Mutation provides the basis for genotypic variability. Sexual reproduction creates new gene combinations by (1) crossing over, (2) random assortment of homologous chromosomes, and (3) outbreeding.

12   All the genes present in a population constitute its gene pool. In large, randomly breeding populations, the frequency of each gene in the gene pool remains constant (Hardy-Weinberg law).

13   Populations produce more young than the number which would replace the parental population. If, as is usually the case, the environment already is supporting as large a population as it can, the offspring will be subjected to a "struggle for existence." Any gene or gene combination that increases the likelihood that an individual will (1) survive to sexual maturity, (2) mate, and (3) raise larger families will be favored. This is natural selection.

14   In addition, the gene pool of a population can be altered by (1) migration of genes from other populations into it and (2) sampling errors when the population is small (drift).

15   Behavior that leads to the death of an individual may nonetheless be selected for if that behavior promotes the welfare of close relatives of the victim (kin selection).

16   Natural selection may affect the distribution of phenotypes in a population in three ways: (1) stabilizing selection—in which individuals at each extreme are selected against; (2) directional selection—in which individuals at one extreme are selected for while those at the other extreme are selected against; (3) disruptive selection—in which individuals at both extremes are favored over those near the mean.

17   Speciation is the formation of one or more descendant species from a single ancestral species. In most, if not all, cases it requires that the ancestral species become separated into two or more geographically isolated subpopulations upon which natural selection and/or drift act differently to form distinctive gene pools. If and when two incipient species become reunited, they may resume interbreeding and reform a single gene pool. Alternatively, one or more isolating mechanisms may prevent successful interbreeding. In the latter case, intense competition between them is likely to promote directional selection which reduces the intensity of the competition. Ultimately, a time is reached when the two new species are generally incapable of successful interbreeding. Speciation is complete.

BUILDING READING SKILLS _____

1. In paragraph 9: "We believe that all our present species have diverged from common ancestors and initially from a single, first form of life." What is the implication of this statement for the human species?

2. The processes of adaptation to the environment and the formation of new species are discussed without giving examples of actual living animals or plants. Try to find some illustrations of a living species' adaptation to its environment, either animal or plant, by looking at other books or in an encyclopedia. Share your findings with others in your group.

TALKING/WRITING ABOUT _____

1. In a group, discuss why you believe 'The Origin of the Species' has had such an impact on the world. What other books have influenced peoples' beliefs about themselves and their place in the universe?

2. A famous court trial took place in the United States in the 1920's which involved Darwin's theories of evolution. Later, a play was written about that trial entitled *Inherit the Wind*, by Jerome Lawrence. Try to obtain a copy in your school or local library. After reading *Inherit the Wind*, write a summary of the plot.

3. What do you know about the current debate in the United States over so-called "scientific creationism?" Share your information with the others. What does it have to do with the play, *Inherit the Wind*?

Characteristics of the Organizational Behavior Field

BEFORE READING

To Think About:

1. Remember that this selection was taken from a textbook which discussed many aspects of the field of organizational behavior. What academic department, school, or faculty might use a book about organizational behavior?

2. Skim the first two paragraphs. The first one defines "scientific behavior," followed by a breakdown of the main points. Then there is a diagram (called "a figure"). Without reading these paragraphs in full, mark the three parts by putting a check (√) in the margin.

3. Skim the three short paragraphs following the diagram (p. 3, 4, 5). Underline the word or word groups which begin each paragraph. What do you expect these paragraphs to contain?

    a) a story

    b) a report

    c) a description of an example

4. The section titled 'Managers in Action' is a mini case-study. What do you think it will be about?

    a) a story about a manager using the scientific method successfully

    b) a story about someone who could not use the scientific method efficiently

    c) an unrelated story which will help readers make a comparison between theory and practice

Now, use the Guided Reading Activities as you read the selection.

GUIDED READING ACTIVITIES ————

1. In paragraph 1, find the key sentence. It gives a definition of the scientific method. Underline it.

2. In paragraph 1: Can you guess the meaning of the popular expression, "to wing it?" Notice that the sentence compares two kinds of behavior.
    a) to use the scientific method
    b) to carry out a task without a plan or without preparation
    c) to use specially trained birds

3. In paragraphs 3, 4, 5: Find at least three characteristics of the scientific method. To do so, look for the words: *first, second, finally*.

    Write your answers below:

    _____

    _____

    _____

    _____

    _____

Characteristics of the Organizational Behavior Field

by P. Hunsacker and C. Cook

A SCIENTIFIC METHOD

1 The **scientific method** of studying organizational behavior and implementing its principles in the workplace is a fairly natural part of the job for many managers. What it basically amounts to is this: By systematically gathering and analyzing information, a manager is able to establish general behavioral laws that lead to reliable predictions of future events and timely interventions at the appropriate levels. "Systematically" is the key word. The fact that some managerial performance records are better than others can often be explained by the successful managers' application of the scientific method as compared with their less successful counterparts' tendency to "wing it."

2 Figure 1.2 is a simple diagram of how the scientific method is applied to organizational behavior. Essentially it is a four-stage procedure:

1. Observing facts about the real-world behavior of individuals, groups, and organizations.

2. Formulating explanations of these phenomena through the *inductive* process.

3. Making predictions and hypotheses about the real-world phenomena through the *deductive* process.

4. Verifying the predictions and hypotheses by means of systematic, controlled experiments.

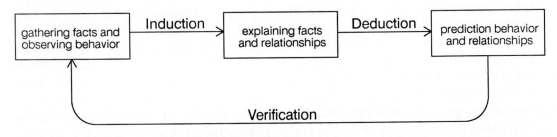

Figure 1.2 The scientific method. Based on Eugene F. Stone. *Research Methods in Organizational Behavior* (Glenview, Ill.: Scott, Foresman, 1978).

3   In the section below, Managers in Action, Jodie Ross's application of the scientific method in her performance evaluations demonstrates several important aspects of this approach. First, instead of focusing on a single event, in a one-shot measurement of performance, this manager studies multiple events—in several performance areas—over the entire year. If only one event were selected for observation, an employee's rare "off day" might lead to an erroneous conclusion; and if only one dimension of behavior were studied, the conclusion might be equally misleading.

4   Second, data is gathered systematically over an entire year in each of the criterion areas for all the new employees. This aspect of the scientific approach guards against the biases that often arise when judgments are based on undocumented hindsight or "overall impressions." When specific data is *not* recorded and maintained, it's easy to be influenced by recollections of extreme behavior that was unusually outstanding or inferior.

5   Finally, the scientific method places some control on extraneous variables that may influence the observed behavior; this results in more reliable and more valid inferences. Controlling the frequency of and the circumstances surrounding the observations justified greater confidence in the interpretations.

——— Managers in Action ———
The Scientific Method in Performance Appraisal

6 Jodie Ross is manager of the High-Tech Unit of Carbondale Research Institute. Among her responsibilities is a first-year performance evaluation of all new employees in the unit. Jodie approaches this task by gathering factual information throughout the year about each new employee's behavior and its results: the quantity and quality of written reports, effectiveness of interaction with coworkers on project teams, degree of initiative demonstrated on projects, and effectiveness in making presentations to clients and top management.

7   She measures and analyzes each employee's performance against her preestablished expectations and standards for these areas of behavior. Then she draws some conclusions about how effective their overall performance has been. Based on these conclusions regarding past performance, Jodie goes on to predict how well each new employee will perform in the future and to plan specific career-development programs for each of them. Jodie follows the same data-gathering and measuring procedure during the subsequent year to verify the accuracy of her predictions and the effectiveness of her development prescriptions.

BUILDING READING SKILLS ━━━━━━━━

1. Make a list of ten terms connected with organizational behavior which appear in the selection. Give each a definition according to the content presented in the selection.

    1. _____   6. _____

    2. _____   7. _____

    3. _____   8. _____

    4. _____   9. _____

    5. _____   10. _____

2. Redraw the diagram in Figure 1.2 on page 67 and fill the boxes with the details from the Jodie Ross case-study. What happened during each phase?
    gathering facts   *explaining facts*   *predicting*

3. How was the verification phase carried out?

TALKING/WRITING ABOUT ━━━━━━━━

1. Discuss the features of the scientific method presented in the selection. Is it general enough to suit other contexts beyond management organization? Can it be applied to a field with which you are acquainted?

2. Do you know someone who is a manager? The person may work in a business or industry where there are at least ten employees. It may be a person who has a staff or administrative job in your school or college. Carry out a mini field-study in which you find out what that person does on the job. To do so you will need to interview the person as well as observe him or her in the workplace. Keep field notes of your interviews and observations. They will become your source of information for writing a brief case-study about the person. Use the 'Managers in Action' section on page 68 as a model.

The Eye, the Brain, and the Computer: Artificial Intelligence

BEFORE READING

To Think About:

1. What do you already know about artificial intelligence?

2. Are you acquainted with any one of the examples given in paragraph 1 of an inanimate object being turned into a "human-like" person? Have you ever seen a motion picture about a "Frankenstein" monster? Share your experiences with the others in your group.

3. From your own experience, what can a computer do?

4. Skim 'Artificial Intelligence.' What are the four subtitles?

_____

_____

_____

_____

What viewpoint do you expect to find in the selection?
a) the limitations of computers
b) the endless possibilities in computers

Vocabulary Preparation

Key words and expressions contain main ideas. Usually, it is important to know them before reading the selection. For example, *artificial intelligence* is a key expression. Another one is:

paradigm   a pattern, example, or model

Now, use the Guided Reading Activities as you read the selection.

GUIDED READING ACTIVITIES ━━━━━━━━━━━━

1. In 'The Mechanization of Thought:' This section contains three paragraphs. Below are possible subtitles for each of them. Find the most suitable subtitle for each. Write the number of the paragraph in the blank.
    a) The reasoning ability of the mind and artificial intelligence _____
    b) The limitations of artificial intelligence _____
    c) Examples of mechanically recreated human-like thinking and behavior as they appear in literature _____
    d) The history of the development of mechanical reasoning _____
    e) Unsuccessful attempts in recreating human intelligence _____

2. In 'The Computer and the Two Paradigms:' The two paradigms are a) the sequential paradigm, and b) the global paradigm. To what extent have each of these two paradigms been developed in computers? Use the space below to write your answers:

    a) _____

    b) _____

3. Paragraph 5 gives an example of how the computer can be more effective than the human brain. Do you know of other examples?

4. In 'How Can We Distinguish Between Mechanical and Intelligent Behavior:' What is the main idea in this section? Can a computer program appear "intelligent" to an outside observer? Be ready to explain to your partner or small group.

5. In 'The Role of Representation in Intelligent Behavior:' What does the stick configuration problem on page 74 prove? Be ready to explain it to your partner or small group.

6. In 'Summary and Discussion:' There are many questions which still need to be answered with respect to AI. List the three most important questions according to your viewpoint.

    _____

    _____

    _____

The Eye, the Brain, and the Computer: Artificial Intelligence

by M. Fischler and O. Firschein

THE MECHANIZATION OF THOUGHT

1 The idea of man converting an inanimate object into a "human-like" thinking entity is an old one. In Greek myth we have the story of Pygmalion, a king of Cyprus who fashions a female figure of ivory that was brought to life by Aphrodite. In the Golem legend of the late sixteenth century, Rabbi Löw of Prague breathes life into a figure of clay. In the nineteenth century there is the story of the scientist Frankenstein, who creates a living creature.

2 Formal investigation of the limits of mechanical reasoning did not occur until the twentieth century. Alan Turing, a British mathematician, carried out investigations using a conceptual model that he called an automaton (now known as a Turing machine). In the 1950s, Turing was able to prove formally that there is a "universal automaton" that can simulate the performance of any other automaton if it is given an appropriate description of that automaton. In addition, Turing proved that certain types of automata could never be built, e.g., one that could tell whether an arbitrary program run on an arbitrary automaton would ever halt.

3 In recent years, the information processing paradigm has become a popular model for explaining the reasoning ability of the human mind. As stated by Simon [Simon 81], "At the root of intelligence are symbols, with their denotative power and their susceptibility to manipulation . . . and symbols can be manufactured of almost anything that can be arranged and patterned and combined." This view, that intelligence is independent of the mechanisms by which the symbol processing is accomplished, is held by most researchers in the field of artificial intelligence.

THE COMPUTER AND THE TWO PARADIGMS

4 The digital computer is the only device that has been used to achieve any significant degree of artificial (machine) intelligence. However, the conventional digital computer is a sequential symbol manipulator, and is primarily suitable for tasks that can be broken down into a series of simple steps. Thus, it is only effective for realizing one of the two basic paradigms employed in human intelligence: the sequential paradigm. Attempts to duplicate human abilities involving the

global (gestalt) paradigm, such as visual perception, have been strikingly inferior, even for visual tasks that people consider extremely simple.

5   At the present time there is a vast difference in favor of the human brain, as compared to the computer, with respect to logical complexity, memory characteristics, and learning ability. Computer-based AI must be specialized to very restricted domains to be at all comparable to human performance. For example, games with a limited number of positions and possible moves are well matched to the computer's great search speed and infallible memory.

HOW CAN WE DISTINGUISH BETWEEN MECHANICAL AND INTELLIGENT BEHAVIOR?

6 Two basic attributes of intelligence are learning and understanding. One might think that an artificial device possessing these capabilities is indeed intelligent. However, we can illustrate the presence of both of these attributes in the very limited context of a coin-matching game. In this example, the computer *learns* the playing pattern of its opponent, and in practice will beat almost all human opponents who are not familiar with the details of the program. The computer demonstrates its *understanding* of the game situation by its outstanding ability to predict the opponent's moves.

7   However, the computer starts with the key elements of its later understanding, since the programmer has provided the model of choosing heads or tails based on the statistics of the

opponent's previous four-move patterns. The only active role played by the program is to collect the statistics of play, and to make choices based on these statistical data. To the outside observer the program seems intelligent, but once we examine its actual details we see that it is quite simple and mechanical. Some might point out that this same argument can also be applied to human performance; it is conceivable that most of the basic models necessary for intelligent performance are inborn, and all we do is select the proper model and adjust the parameters.

THE ROLE OF REPRESENTATION IN INTELLIGENT BEHAVIOR

8 As indicated in the previous section, a paradigm is an overall approach for dealing with a class of problems. One of the most critical elements in the specific realization of a paradigm is the *form* in which the relevant knowledge is encoded.

To illustrate the role played by the selected representation in solving a problem, consider the example depicted in Fig. 1-4, which shows a configuration of 17 sticks. The problem is to remove five sticks so as to leave three squares with no extra sticks remaining. You are required to find all such solutions! You might try to find one such solution before you read further.

9   If the primitive element you manipulate in searching for a solution is the individual stick, and you remove five sticks at a time and check the result, then even if you are careful not

Figure 1-4 The Stick Configuration Problem: the Role of Representation in Problem Solving.

The problem is to remove five sticks so as to leave three of the original squares with no extra sticks, and to do this in all possible ways.

to repeat a particular trial twice, you must make over 6000 trials to be sure that you have found all possible solutions. (There are about 6000 combinations of 17 sticks taken 5 at a time.)

10   If the primitive element you manipulate is a square, you can select three squares at a time and retain the configuration if there are exactly five sticks left to be removed. Then there are only 20 unique configurations that must be examined to find all solutions, and there is a 300:1 reduction in the number of trials over the approach based on representing the given configuration as a collection of individual sticks. (There are 20 combinations of 6 squares taken 3 at a time.)

11   Finally, we note that there are 17 sticks, and after removing five, the remaining 12 can form three squares only if these squares are noncontiguous (i.e., have no sides in common). It is easily seen that there are only two configurations of three noncontiguous squares, and both of these are valid solutions. Here, by using a representation that allowed us to employ deductive reasoning, the required effort is reduced by a factor of 3000:1.

SUMMARY AND DISCUSSION

12   Intelligence is more an open collection of attributes than it is a single well-defined entity. Some of the attributes most closely identified with intelligence are learning, reasoning, understanding, linguistic competence, purposeful behavior, and effective interaction with the environment (including perception). Since intelligence has no clear definition, differing theories of intelligence are not necessarily in conflict, but often differ mainly in the assumed definition of intelligence as either (1) a natural phenomenon appearing in living organisms, especially man, or (2) an arbitrarily specified set of abilities.

13   Most psychological theories of intelligence are what might be called "performance theories" since they are based on measurements of performance in specified skills, and make assertions about the relationships and correlations between different tests of performance. For example, correlations between tests have been used by investigators attempting to determine

if human intelligence is the result of a single coherent mechanism or a collection of loosely integrated independent processes. Such theories are largely empirical and offer very little insight into the nature of intelligence. Most of our concern in the later portions of this book is with understanding how specified abstract structures can produce intelligent behavior.

14   Intelligence tests, whether for people or machines, have some practical utility, but cannot be expected to accurately measure an undefinable quantity. Another complicating factor in our understanding of intelligence is the role played by consciousness, and the relation between mind and brain.

15   It is possible to assume that most intelligent behavior arises from one of two distinct paradigms (strategies): In the sequential (or logical) paradigm, a single path is found which links available knowledge and evidence to some desired conclusion; in the parallel (gestalt) paradigm, all connections between evidence and possible conclusions are appraised simultaneously. There is some evidence that the human brain has separate specialized machinery for each of these two paradigms.

16   A key insight provided by work in artificial intelligence is that intelligent behavior not only requires stored knowledge and methods for manipulating this knowledge, but is critically dependent on the relationship between the specific encoding of the knowledge and the purpose for which this knowledge is used. This concept, the central role of representation in intelligent behavior, is one of our major themes.

17 **The Ultimate Limits of AI.** We have briefly sketched the nature of human and machine intelligence. In later chapters we will repeatedly return to the questions, "What can a machine know about the world in which it exists?" and "What are the mechanisms needed to acquire, understand, and employ such knowledge?" We will also address a number of basic questions concerning the limits and ultimate role of machine intelligence:

18 • Can man create a machine more intelligent than himself?

• Are there components of man's intelligence that cannot be found in any animal or duplicated in a machine?

• Can all intelligent behavior be duplicated by the current approach to AI, namely by decomposing a given problem into a sequence of simple tasks or subproblems that can be precisely stated and solved?

• Can a machine ever exhibit fully human behavior without having been human and thus properly socialized? In a more limited sense, is human intelligence in some way bound up in the *human experience* or even human heredity?

• Is intelligent behavior realizable, or even conceivable, with the type of computing instruments currently available?

• Is intelligent behavior in some way a property of organic structure, and thus not achievable by nonorganic machinery?

TALKING/WRITING ABOUT ⎯⎯⎯⎯⎯⎯⎯⎯⎯⎯

1. Try to describe the year 2025. What will computers be able to do? Share your ideas with others in your group.

2. What are the limitations of using the information processing paradigm as "a . . . model for explaining the reasoning ability of the human mind?" (paragraph 3) For example, how does it account for unconscious thinking, hunches, intuitions, etc.? Brainstorm the topic with a small group. Then, write a short composition explaining your own ideas.

Global Environment and the Social Fabric after Nuclear War

BEFORE READING

To Think About:

1. What period of time does the title refer to? How do we know?
   a) recorded past
   b) on-going present
   c) potential future

2. What can we expect will be discussed and described in this article based on the information in the title? Choose two from the following four:
   a) illnesses which could result from nuclear war
   b) changes which could take place in our physical environment
   c) changes which might take place in the social structure and our value systems
   d) changes that might take place in human interpersonal interaction

3. The first of the two authors, Philip Morrison, is a famous physicist who participated in the testing and combat use of the atomic bomb. How might that fact affect his viewpoint?

4. The selection starts with a brief abstract. The purpose of an abstract is to give the reader the main ideas and conclusions in a brief, focused, and concentrated manner. An abstract, therefore, is packed with information and key terms. If you understand the abstract, you are prepared for reading the full article.

Vocabulary Preparation

The following are key terms:

calculate	1) extrapolate; estimate 2) compute by using arithmetic
estimate	make a judgment based on approximate calculation
extrapolate	estimate beyond what is known based on the present knowledge
determine	calculate precisely
fabric	a framework or structure
global	pertaining to the whole world

Now, use the Guided Reading Activities as you read the selection.

GUIDED READING ACTIVITIES ————————————————

1. Answer the following questions based on the information in the abstract at the beginning of the selection.
    a) What can be calculated roughly?
    b) What are the extrapolations based upon? (two things)
    c) What can only be crudely estimated?
    d) What can never be adequately determined?

2. The following adverbs are used to describe the level of accuracy with which the calculations are done. The list presents a scale from highly to less accurate:

    high   *low*

    precisely,   accurately,   adequately,   roughly,   crudely,   inaccurately

    Copy out all the instances in the abstract where any of these adverbs are used together with the appropriate verb with which it occurs:

    example   *line*

    _____

    _____

    _____

    _____

3. The first paragraph states that two distinct aspects of the effects of nuclear war will be discussed. What are they?

    _____

    _____

4. Read the subtitles of the whole article. There are two main ones which refer back to the two aspects mentioned in paragraph 1. They are:

    _____and

    _____

    There are three lower level subtitles that refer to elements of environmental effects. They are:

    _____   _____ and

    _____.

    There is also a final section which summarizes the article. It is titled:

    _____

Global Environment and the Social Fabric after Nuclear War

by Philip Morrison and Jack Dennis

Some environmental effects months after a massive exchange of nuclear warheads can be calculated roughly by extrapolation from nuclear test explosions and volcanic eruptions; other effects can only be estimated crudely. Radioactive fallout will increase the incidence of cancers of all kinds, dust may drastically reduce agricultural output because of climatic changes, and the ozone layer of the stratosphere might be severely reduced, causing a five- to ten-fold increase in the ultraviolet radiation reaching the earth's surface. How far such a change would disturb the biosphere may never be adequately determined.

The character of society after the millions of dead are buried—or abandoned—is difficult to predict. Physical and psychological trauma will persist, aggravated by severe shortages of food, water, fuel, medicines, and medical care. The accumulated culture of our species may not survive a full-scale nuclear war.

1 WHAT ARE THE EFFECTS of nuclear war that extend in time and space beyond destruction of target cities and decimation of targeted populations? Two distinct aspects on this question are: (A) the effects of nuclear war on the whole natural environment as habitat for biological species, including the remaining human population; and (B) the viability of the rent fabric of human society.

(Continued on page 81.)

GUIDED READING ACTIVITIES (cont.) ━━━━━

5. Read the introductory section 'Environmental Effects.' It contains four paragraphs. Write down the first sentence of each:

p. 2: _____

_____

p. 3: _____

_____

p. 4: _____

_____

p. 5: _____

_____

Notice that paragraphs 2 and 3 start with sentences about experience. Read them to discover what experience the authors are talking about.

Paragraph 4 deals with the potential effect of a nuclear attack as opposed to a full-scale war. What is an example of such effects?

Paragraph 5 in this section sets out the next three paragraphs. They will deal with:

_____, _____, and

_____.

6. In 'Fallout:' In what sequence do the following events occur? Place a number in front of each.

_____ a) some fallout reaches the ground months after the explosion
_____ b) debris of the bomb and its target are sent up in the rising fireball
_____ c) the deposit falls on the ground nearby

7. In 'Dust:' Be ready to explain to your partner or small group:
What have we learned from the natural explosion of volcanoes?

8. In 'Ozone:' While reading, think of the following questions. Answer them immediately after reading:
a) How damaging can the ultraviolet light from the sun be to human beings and to plants?
b) How does the ozone layer protect us?
c) How might the ozone layer be affected by massive detonation?

ENVIRONMENTAL EFFECTS

2   From direct experience we know some limits on the global effects of nuclear weapons detonations. Between 1945 and 1963, and to a limited extent thereafter, the nuclear powers conducted an unintended experiment bearing on this topic, for they set off test nuclear explosions in the open air, at the surface of the sea, undersea, and even at the edge of space, until the prohibition of such tests by the Partial Test Ban Treaty signed at Moscow in 1963. Up to the time of signing, there had been about 380 nuclear explosions that threw up material into the atmosphere.

3   Extrapolating from this experience to the consequences of nuclear war is difficult for several reasons. We do not know much about the design features of the various weapons detonated, whose contributions to fallout vary with the details of their makeup; at present, all we have to go on are estimates by various expert groups of the total energy yield of all test explosions open to the atmosphere—somewhere in the range of 350 to 530 megatons.

4   The more significant factor, however, is the size of this total, which is roughly equivalent to that of a small nuclear attack, not to a full-scale war between the superpowers. All-out nuclear war is now estimated to yield between twenty and thirty times the total release from all earlier tests in the open air. That there have been global effects from even the smaller amount is certain; we can be sure, for example, that many individuals worldwide have suffered the induction of a fatal tumor from the fallout, although we cannot say just who or how many they are.

5   The major consequences are threefold, resulting from fallout, the production of dust, and the depletion of the ozone layer in the upper atmosphere.

6 **Fallout**   Fallout is the deposit of radioactive material on the ground from the debris of bomb and target sent into the heights within the rising fireball after the explosion. The finer the dust particles on which the radioactive atoms have lodged, the slower the rate of fallout. Much of the fission product, the chief type of radioactivity from the bomb, is deposited nearby, falling to the ground within hours at most. This defines the local fallout which forms the so-called plume, blown downwind like the plume of smoke from an industrial chimney. But here we are concerned with fallout after months of time, not just a few hours.

7 **Dust**   The second major worldwide effect is the lifting of dust particles up to the stratosphere by the explosions. This dust has most of the radioactive effects we have described, but it has others as well. The most evident consequence of dust in the upper air is the effect on the incoming sunlight. We know of this phenomenon, unlike the radioactive effects, not from the bomb tests so much as from the natural explosions of volcanos.

8 **Ozone**   It is well known that biologically damaging ultraviolet light, with wavelengths between about 310 nanometers and 290 nanometers, is copiously emitted by the sun. These rays

(Continued on page 83.)

GUIDED READING ACTIVITIES (cont.) ━━━━━━

9. In 'The Social Fabric:' Consider the damaging effects of a potential nuclear war that are described. After reading the entire section, write a brief summary of the main effects. Categorize them under the following:

a) immediate effects (right after explosion or attack)

b) housing difficulties and its effects

c) energy shortage and its effects

d) food shortage and its effects

e) possible changes in government

are not penetrating: their effects are at the skin surface, though often important. Skin cancer, snow blindness (a sunburn of the outer layers of the eye), sunburn of exposed skin, and increased vitamin D production are effects known in humans and other animals. Plants are also affected; various agricultural crops, more the broad-leaved ones like peas, beans, or tomatoes, tend to lose chlorophyll and grow less well. Most of this radiation, however, does not reach the lower atmosphere because of a photochemical reaction in the thin air of the stratosphere and above; as a result of this photochemical reaction, the substance ozone is formed, which absorbs the radiation in question. The ozone layer, as it is called, is in a state of dynamic equilibrium, which massive detonation of nuclear weaponry will surely disrupt, although the extent of the disturbance is uncertain.

9   What is sure is that the strongly heated air of a thermonuclear fireball undergoes chemical reactions that produce some amount of the several oxides of nitrogen. If these rise into the ozone layer, they may act to reduce the ozone that is present, thus allowing more of the biologically active ultraviolet rays to pass to the surface of the earth. Early estimates suggested that the full-scale explosions we are considering would send enough of the active nitrogen compounds into the upper air to reduce the ozone content very appreciably for a matter of several years before natural elimination of the new materials. But the chemistry is complex. With a great deal of uncer-

tainty, estimates were offered that the ozone might be reduced by as much as 30 to 70 percent in the Northern Hemisphere, rather less in the Southern Hemisphere. This effect would increase the exposure of the living forms of the earth to this radiation by a factor of five or ten times.

THE SOCIAL FABRIC

10   After a nuclear attack, the immediate effects will all be over in one or two months. The fires will have burnt out. Most of the myriads of victims of blast injury and burns will either have died or at least partially recovered. Those suffering acute radiation sickness from direct radiation or from intense early fallout will either be dead or able to survive for years.

11   Outside the ruins, immediate problems of survival will concern controlling infection, providing water supply and sanitary services, reestablishing some kind of communications, and avoiding needless deaths from inadvertent exposure to fallout radiation in many contaminated areas.

12   The loss of housing would be immense since many survivors would be from areas where homes had been destroyed by blast and fire. A communal life-style would be thrust upon the surviving refugees of urban areas. Masses of people will attempt to escape from target areas both before and after an attack; the number of refugees from all urban areas might reach 50 to 100 million persons, an unprecedented number.

13   How will the economic and social structure of an attacked country survive? History provides us with little useful guidance. The yield of the bombs dropped on Japan was tiny in comparison with the megatons now carried by intercontinental missiles. More important, these were attacks on a single city by a single weapon—not the near-simultaneous destruction of many cities in a massive attack.

14   In the case of Hiroshima, electricity was restored in some less-damaged areas on the day following the attack, train service to the city was resumed on the next day, certain streetcar lines were operating on the third day, and telephone communications were restored in some sections within ten days. This rapid recovery of some basic services was made possible by the availability of human and material resources from unstricken areas.

15   In World War II, German cities, in particular, were subject to repeated massive bombing raids. Yet the interval between attacks provided an opportunity for conscious or unconscious adjustment to conditions. People improvised and experimented; they achieved a semblance of normal life between the repeated shocks, making it possible to better cope with each successive blow. Even so, the social, political, and economic effects of strategic bombing in World War II were severe. After the war, the revival of the damaged cities was accomplished with large infusions of U.S. capital through the Marshall Plan and with assistance from other outside sources. With the explosion of many strategic warheads against cities, the suddenness and extent of the devastation would be so great that neither the single-weapon attacks on Hiroshima and Nagasaki nor the protracted strategic bombing of Germany and Japan in World War II provide a basis for estimating the consequences. Within an attacked area the change from a normal to a devastated environment will be abrupt and all-encompassing.[5] Life after nuclear war would certainly be very different for the survivors. The banking system and currency would be in desperate disarray. The commodities in demand would be those essential for survival—food, water, shelter from the elements, and energy for space heating. Many industries, even if their plants survived, would find their starting materials absent, labor gone, products irrelevant to the postwar society. They would have to adapt or shut down. Those businesses providing basic materials from local resources would flourish, such as bakeries with stores of flour. Barter would become the usual way of transacting business. Many people would find their former jobs irrelevant. Those who were adaptive or had a variety of skills could readily find productive work, but people who were narrowly trained or had limited skill would be forced into menial work to subsist. In regions where resources were very scarce these people would perish or become dependent on others. Many would become outlaws, preying on the successful survivors.

16   In the United States there is a very efficient but complex and widespread

national food distribution system. Following a major nuclear attack, a considerable area of farmland would be unusable for at least several seasons because of fallout. The scarcity of energy would lead to a scarcity of fertilizer which would further reduce farm productivity for prewar crops, especially wheat. While the nationwide railroad system would be workable, given some fuel, getting grain to the decimated population would be a problem of local distribution and fair division of the supplies. How would the farmers be paid for their grain? If urban areas and their residents are destroyed, the large fraction of the population living in suburban areas and in the countryside would turn to locally grown produce. Obtaining adequate protein would be a serious problem for many people incapable of growing the appropriate crops. Fresh milk, depending on a rapid local delivery system, would be a scarce and expensive commodity; maybe powdered milk could be produced.

17   Much food from farms would be contaminated with fission products from fallout—strontium-90 and cesium-137. Since the health danger is the ill-defined, long-term increase in the incidence of cancer, many people would prefer to accept the risk rather than starve.

18   Severe local food shortages—even winter famine, especially in northern regions—are likely to occur. Conflicts are sure to arise between the central government attempting to send relief to areas of famine and the residents of local regions trying, in a diminished economy, to provide for their own. Such conflicts were seen on a smaller scale, even in the less-damaged states of World War II.

19   The fullest attack postulated would not destroy all sources of energy; a fraction of the electric power plants would survive and some petroleum refining capacity. On the other hand, the cities and the manufacturing industries are large consumers of energy, and their destruction would remove much demand for energy. A large portion of all motor vehicles would probably be destroyed. Commuting to the city would largely disappear. Air conditioning and office lighting would be irrelevant. People would hang clothes outside to dry. The problem would be to manage the distribution of the remaining energy resources to the points of need. The major energy requirement for survival would be for home and apartment heating in severe winter regions; from New York to Denver and beyond, there would be much space heating using wood. The electric grid would be important and relatively easy to restore to, say, one-tenth to one-fourth its former capacity—more might not be necessary for the dwindled, immobilized, only semi-industrialized nation that remains.

20   Our modern, industrial society has become far more interdependent since World War II. If all large urban areas were struck in one attack, it is possible that the entire technical capacity to produce some high-technology products—lasers, for example—would be lost. Perhaps more crucial to survival, many stocks of replacement parts re-

quired to repair and maintain machinery and equipment would be wiped out, forcing cannibalization of some equipment to keep the rest in operation. Much sophisticated equipment—medical equipment, electronic apparatus, and computer-based systems—would more or less quickly fall out of use. The skills to maintain and operate it would be forgotten and not soon recovered.

21   A large portion of universities, professional personnel, and research laboratories are concentrated in the urban areas of the United States. The most extensive collections of written human knowledge are in the libraries of our great cities and universities. A large part of this knowledge and expertise would be lost in a nuclear attack on the cities. Of course, if just one major city or center of learning were spared, the knowledge could be recovered and redistributed—if it were seen to be relevant. If the destruction were so great that most technical products of our society fell out of use, and knowledge of them were not transmitted to succeeding generations, it is possible that the knowledge would not be regained.

22   It is questionable whether the federal government would survive a massive nuclear attack. At some level of damage, the remaining population would be so poor, and central government services so irrelevant to their lives, that support for past major functions of the central government (such as maintaining military superiority or providing a massive welfare system at high tax cost) would vanish.

23   Very likely new regional systems of governance would form based on common economic interests and the existence of strong leadership. In some areas, banditry and lawlessness would reign instead.

CONCLUSIONS

24   There is no doubt that the international catastrophe of large-scale nuclear war would be of unmatched damage to the target states and to their near neighbors, worse than any famine, war, or pestilence yet witnessed. No mere local events, like volcanos, floods, or earthquakes, compare at all with its continental scope, or its foreseeable 100 or 200 million deaths. For the physical effects on the world as a whole, it seems prudent to say that another factor of 10 beyond a 10-thousand megaton exchange would imply very damaging worldwide effects indeed to the human species and to its environment, not excluding the near-extinction of our kind. On the present yield scale, we are at risk of the unknown. We have no prudent safety factors left for events that have so universal an impact. No other such danger to public health has ever come so close to the foreseeable margin. At the same time it is not possible to point to sure worldwide disaster from a great-power nuclear exchange on present scale, though indeed there would be intense suffering everywhere, eventual deaths by the tens of millions, and above all, a desperate gamble for our entire species.

TALKING/WRITING ABOUT ────────────

1. Discuss in your group: Do you agree with the strong points that the writers make? Why?

2. Do you know of any examples of a more regional explosion that had effects of the kind described here?

3. What should be done in order to prevent such cataclysmic events? What organizations do you know about that work to prevent nuclear wars? Try to obtain some of their materials to share with others in your group. Brainstorm ideas for preventing use of nuclear armaments.

READING
FEATURE
STORIES

UNIT INTRODUCTION

READING FEATURE STORIES ━━━━━━━━━

Feature stories appear in newspapers and newsmagazines, but they do not contain the latest news. Instead, they allow writers a chance to explore timely ideas in greater depth than in a regular news story. As a newspaper reader, you can add to your background knowledge of current topics by reading the feature stories. You will find that all of the feature stories in Unit Three are thematically related to topics in the other four Units, so in reading them you will be adding to what you already know.

As a reader, you can expect that a feature story has been written to inform and possibly entertain you. In fact, the writers of some feature stories contribute to the paper regularly. Their readers look for their columns like waiting to hear from good friends. Unit Three contains articles by two such columnist-writers, Jack Smith and Ellen Goodman.

While reading Unit Three, think about adjusting your reading to fit the material at hand. Remember that all reading is not the same. At times, you need to read closely in order to remember facts and information. But there are other kinds of reading as well. It depends on both your purpose for reading and the material.

Some of the selections in Unit Three were written to be read quickly; you will understand the main points after the first reading. Others, however, require close reading of each section or paragraph. Therefore, they require reading strategies that are similar to those you used for reading textbooks in Unit Two. Throughout Unit Three, the activities will guide you into using appropriate reading strategies for each selection.

Does Civilization Owe a Debt to Beer?

A Note About . . .

The author, a *New York Times* feature writer, found the material for this article by reading a journal published by a university anthropology museum. In his reading, he discovered a fascinating account of early man's settlement. He used the information and ideas in the technical article to write a feature story for a general audience.

BEFORE READING

To Think About:

1. The title contains the word "civilization." In a dictionary, you will find that "civilization" means: an advanced stage of development of a group, nation, or of the whole world. In this title, the word refers to the advancement or the development of the human species.

2. "To owe a debt" usually means to owe money. As you read the article, think about what the phrase refers to in this context. Does it mean owing a debt of money?

3. The article contains information about brewing, or the making of beer. You may want to use an encyclopedia or unabridged dictionary to read further about the process.

Vocabulary Preparation

As you read the article, look for the key words in #2 below. If they are unfamiliar, add them to your Personal Vocabulary–Building Notebook.

1. The scientist presented a **hypothesis**, he presented his best ideas or explanation of the question. However, he had no hard evidence. He **hypothesized** that civilization owes a debt to beer.

2. When scientists have opinions or ideas about things but do not have hard evidence or proof for their opinions, they use verbs like those listed below. All of them are used in the article.

   assert   **argue**   **contend**   **favor** (an idea or explanation)

3. The journal in which the original article appeared is written for and by **anthropologists** and **archeologists**. Do you know what each of these social scientists studies? Use your English-English dictionary to make sure you understand the difference between these two fields:

anthropology   archeology

Now, use the Guided Reading Activities as you read the selection.

GUIDED READING ACTIVITIES —————————

1. Paragraph 1 contains a central question of interest to cultural anthropologists. The remainder of the article offers a possible solution to the question, providing arguments for and against the solution. What is the research question which interests anthropologists? Rephrase it in your own words:

   _____

   The answer to this question is important because:
   a) it has tantalized scientists for a long time
   b) it provides information about agriculture, specifically about brewing
   c) it provides an explanation why human beings did not remain hunters but became city dwellers.

2. One word in paragraph 2 tells the reader that the article is based on a scientist's opinion, but the opinion still needs to be proven. What is the word? _____

3. One word in paragraph 3 further reinforces this fact. What is the word?

   _____

4. The anthropologist, Katz, published his article in a journal for anthropologists and archeologists, among others. Why do these two fields have similar interests?

5. Paragraph 4 presents the anthropologist's (Katz) argument according to the writer of the article; it is a paraphrase. Paragraph 5 states the argument in Katz' own words. It is a direct quotation. Find the two versions and compare them. Which words are the same or different?

6. Paragraph 6 contrasts two lifestyles: a) hunting and gathering, b) agricultural. Which one is easier?

   Do the facts follow or go against popular myth or belief (a **myth** can be a popular belief)?

Does Civilization Owe a Debt to Beer?

By William K. Stevens
Special to The New York Times

1 PHILADELPHIA, March 23—Why, 10,000 years or so ago, did people first settle down and go to all the trouble of sowing, cultivating and reaping crops? The question has long tantalized anthropologists and archeologists because once its answer is clear, they will know what sparked the long transformation of humans from wandering hunters into literate city dwellers.

2 Beer did it, argues an anthropologist at the University of Pennsylvania.

3 The event that "primed the pump," according to this new hypothesis, was the accidental discovery by prehistoric humans that wild wheat and barley soaked in water to make gruel, if left out in the open air, did not spoil. In-

stead, natural yeast in the air converted it to a dark, bubbling brew that made whoever drank it feel good. On top of that, the brew made people robust; at the time, it was second only to animal protein as a nutritional source.

4 This combination of mood-altering and nutritional properties would have been incentive enough to cause neolithic hunter-gatherers in the Near East to begin cultivating the grains, Dr. Solomon H. Katz contends in an article published this month in Expedition, the journal of the Museum of Archeology/Anthropology at the University of Pennsylvania.

5 "My argument," Dr. Katz said in an interview, "is that the initial discovery of a stable way to produce alcohol provided

enormous motivation for continuing to go out and collect these seeds and try to get them to do better." The argument is buttressed, Dr. Katz wrote in his article, by the fact that "almost invariably, individuals and societies appear to invest enormous amounts of effort and even risk" in the pursuit of mind-altering foods and beverages.

6 Strong motivation would have been required to break away from the hunting-gathering way of life, according to one view among archeologists, because—contrary to myth—hunting and gathering provided a higher and more reliable standard of living, with less work, than the onerous and often chancy pursuit of agriculture.

(Continued on page 95.)

GUIDED READING ACTIVITIES (cont.) ━━━━━

7. In paragraph 7: The explanation accepted over the last two decades favored environmental and ecological factors for the birth of agriculture. For example, which of the following causes are mentioned?

    _____ population increase   _____ traffic congestion

    _____ food shortages   _____ cultural factors

8. In paragraph 8: When scientists do not agree with each other they bring up "counter-arguments" by expressing their doubts or skepticism. How does Harris express his skepticism? How does he manage not to completely cast doubt on Katz' hypothesis?

9. In paragraphs 9, 10: Explain Harris' counter-argument in your own words:

    _____

    _____

10. Paragraphs 11—15 contain the writer's detailed summary of Katz' hypothesis, including evidence from archeology. Write a brief summary in your own words:

    _____

    _____

    _____

7   Over the last two decades, specialists on the neolithic world have generally favored environmental and ecological explanations for the birth of agriculture. For instance, it has been commonly held that population increases forced neolithic peoples to search for ways to expand the food supply. But now, some scholars are beginning to doubt this explanation and are giving more weight to cultural factors. Dr. Katz's specialty is the study of the development of cuisine, broadly defined, as one such cultural factor.

Earliest evidence of beer drinking in Mesopotamia, circa 4000 B.C., was found on a stamp seal, at Tepe Gawra, in northern Iraq.

8   While Dr. Katz's beer hypothesis is likely to attract interest, skepticism is already being expressed. "I would say it's an ingredient in the mix of causal factors," said Dr. Marvin Harris, an anthropologist at the University of Florida who is a theorist on cultural evolution, "but I wouldn't want to put a kind of prime-mover status" on it.

9   What might have happened, said Dr. Harris, is that after the game animals of the late Pleistocene disappeared and deprived humans of their major source of food, people began combing the environment for anything that would sustain life. "So what do you do with several tons of wild seeds you've just harvested?" he asked. "You settle down in a village and protect it. Meanwhile, the animals are coming closer to the stands of grain, and then there's a gradual transition over to domestication" of both plants and animals. There is probably a "symbiotic relationship" between domestication of the two, he said.

10   "There are plenty of plausible alternatives," he said. The process probably had its "alcoholic aspect," he said, but "the whole thing is a package."

11   Dr. Katz argues that grain-derived alcohol was the critical element. In many cultures, he says, the use of alcohol has been made so central to social and religious practice that any disruption of its supply would be seen as a serious problem. In the Near East, where agriculture and village life first appeared, the need to solve this problem could well have accounted for the

transition from hunting and gathering, he said.

12   The discovery of brewing could have happened quite easily, according to the anthropologist. First, he says, wheat and barley were soaked in water to make gruel. Some of the grains accidentally sprouted; and when tasted, were found to be sweet. For this reason they were saved, and eventually natural yeast in the air mixed with the watery gruel to produce a solution with perhaps 3 to 5 percent alcohol.

13   The archeological record so far provides no direct evidence that beer-making prompted the cultivation of grain, Dr. Katz said. But, he wrote in his article, the beer hypothesis is compatible with one aspect of the record that has puzzled archeologists. At early neolithic village sites where stone tools used for cultivation were found, very few carbonized grain seeds were in evidence. Had they been more plentiful, it would have indicated that grain was used in the baking of bread, as is commonly believed. Since beer making does not require exposing grains to fire, he writes, "It could be an everyday activity and yet produce not a single carbonized seed."

14   Moreover, he said, narrow-necked storage vessels of the kind needed to promote carbonation have been found dating back to the beginnings of neolithic times. "This vessel is so common through the world that it's incredible," he said. "Every time you have one of these narrow necks, you know you've got something that's keeping the air and the oxygen outside and the carbon dioxide inside." The presence of carbon dioxide helped keep the brew acidic, in turn protecting it from the development of toxic qualities that can otherwise occur.

15   By the time the neolithic village culture of the Near East had evolved into the city-states of Sumeria some 5,000 years ago, he said, beer-drinking had been raised to a high status. The world's oldest recipe, written on Sumerian tablets, is for beer. Another tablet contains a hymn to the beer goddess, Ninkasi.

TALKING/WRITING ABOUT ─────────────

1. With a partner or in a small group, discuss these questions:
   a) The writer presents both the hypothesis which Katz proposed and the counter-arguments which Harris raised. Which do you think the author believes? What evidence leads you to your opinion?
   b) How can information obtained by archeologists help anthropologists?

2. If the conditions permit, try an experiment: take equal parts of wild wheat and barley that have soaked in water. Leave the mixture in the open air. Describe to the others in your group what happened. Did the mixture ferment?

   The process you carried out for bringing about fermentation is the one described in the article. When you read about "brewing" in an encyclopedia or dictionary, did you find a different process described? Discuss the similarities or the differences of the processes with the others in your group.

3. Suppose you go to Philadelphia and visit the Museum of Archeology/Anthropology at the University of Pennsylvania. In one of the cases displaying 5,000 year-old Sumerian tablets, you notice that on one of them there is a drawing showing human figures stirring what is stored in a large narrow-necked vessel, similar to the one in the illustration on page 95.

   When you leave the Museum you find that the postcard shop has this drawing on one of the cards for sale. You purchase a card to send to your best friend back home. Write a brief message to your best friend describing what you saw in the Museum and what the illustration on the card represents.

Escape from Time Becomes the Time of Her Life

A Note About . . .

Ellen Goodman's feature stories appear in newspapers throughout North America. Wisely and with wit, she writes about concerns of women and men in society. Often she uses words and phrases that have more than one meaning. Every week she writes to meet a deadline. In this article, she describes how she escaped from time and from deadlines while on a vacation.

BEFORE READING ━━━━━━━━━━━━━━━━━

To Think About:

1. Read the title carefully. The author is on a vacation; she has escaped from deadlines . . . and time. She sends a postcard from Casco Bay, Maine that says: "I'm having the time of my life here." Everyone back home knows she's having a wonderful vacation.

2. Read the dateline carefully: The dateline gives the place where the writer is. What is Goodman's usual dateline? (The place where she is based.) What is the dateline on this article? Locate Maine (Me. is the abbreviation) in an atlas. How far is it from Boston?

To Look For:

Since they have short sentences and brief paragraphs, many feature stories can be read rapidly. They provide excellent practice for reading-in-chunks, or reading to get the meaning of an entire paragraph or groups of paragraphs in a quick eye-scan.

As you read, look for the way in which the writer's voice shifts:

begins with:	I
changes to:	our/we
then shifts to:	he says that
finally goes back to:	my (I)

Vocabulary Preparation

Look out for these expressions as you read:

wind down   to slow down; the author is having fun with words since some wristwatches and clocks require winding.

lose track   to lose one's sense of time.

reckon   "I suppose," or "I think," in regional American dialect. Remember, Goodman is writing from Maine, not from a big city such as Boston.

slip out   to easily move out of a place or to get out of clothing

Now, read the entire selection without looking up words in the dictionary.

Escape From Time Becomes the Time of Her Life

By Ellen Goodman

1 CASCO BAY, Me.—I have taken time off. Literally. The watch that straps my workaday wrist to its demands sits on the kitchen shelf. I have shed its manufactured time, its minute hand, hour hand, just the way I shed my city wardrobe, makeup, panty hose, skirt. Gradually I have even begun to lose track of time. First the minute and then the hour, finally the day. My watch and I have wound down.

2 I reckon that my real vacation starts the moment I forget whether it's Thursday or Friday. And the moment I realize that it doesn't make any difference. At last, I tell myself, I have slipped out of one time frame and sunk into another. I have left a world divided by nothing more than numbers, 60 minutes, 24 hours, seven days a week. I have entered a world of seasons: blueberry, raspberry, blackberry season; lobsters that shed old shells and then harden new ones.

3 My daily life here is connected more to the tide than to the time. At low tide I can harvest the mussels that lie under great heaps of seaweed clinging to rocks by their umbilical beards. At high tide the mackerel may swim in hot pursuit into the cove. The cove is not a store with hours set by its owner.

4 Like most people in the Western world, I have grown up in the artificial environment of modern society. It's a place dominated by external timekeepers, calendars, schedules, clocks. Our lives are subdivided into fiscal years, academic years, weekdays, weekends, deadlines. We are taught that there is a time to get up, a time to go to work, a time to eat. We set the clock by a single standard.

5 Time orders our lives and, inevitably, orders us around. We are so removed from natural rhythms that we rarely confront how "unnatural" this is. How unnatural to strap time on.

6 But we didn't always live with this artificial timing. In "Time Wars," Jeremy Rifkin explains just how recently people have been alienated from their natural rhythms to those of the schedule, the clock and now the computer with its nanosecond culture.

7 The schedule—that control on our lives—was the invention of the Benedictine monks whose early passion for organizing and filling every minute of the day grew from St. Benedict's warning that "idleness is the enemy of the soul." His followers reintroduced the Roman hour and invented the mechanical clock.

8 Not until the 15th Century did clocks, those icons of temporal time, begin to rival churches in the city squares. Not until the 17th Century did clocks have a minute hand. "Me-

dieval time," Rifkin writes, "was still sporadic, leisurely, unpredictable and above all tied to experiences rather than abstract numbers." It was the merchants and factory owners who eventually, and with great difficulty, trained workers—those who had previously lived in accord with the seasons—to become as regular as clockwork.

9   Today, Rifkin writes, "the high achievers see time as an obstacle to overcome, an enemy to defeat. They equate faster and faster learning with victory over time; to win is to beat the clock."

10   Is it any wonder that many of us choose vacations that stretch uninterrupted from sunrise to sunset, choose to re-enter the natural cycle, days of idleness, that friend of the soul? Is it any wonder that we seek, for just a while, not to think of time as a commodity to be spent, saved, wasted, used, but to live from tide to tide?

11   My own escape is hardly complete. A creature of habit more than habitat, I have yet to spend a day without once looking at a clock or asking the hour. My vacation itself is circumscribed. I have only a certain amount of time al-

lotted to timelessness. It will end at a predetermined moment. I will go home according to the boat schedule, write on deadline.

12   But on this day the ghostly white impression left by the watch on my arm has finally browned. I can barely see its imprint on my life.

Ellen Goodman is a syndicated columnist who is based in Boston.

AFTER THE FIRST READING

Check all of the statements below that are true.
In the article, Goodman writes about:

_____ a wristwatch she has taken off while on a holiday

_____ losing track of time, yet she knows there will be another deadline when the holiday is over

_____ her belief that Western society is too tied to clockwatching

_____ the sense of timelessness that comes when one is on a vacation.

Read the selection again. Then go on to the section, Building Reading Skills.

BUILDING READING SKILLS ─────────────

Reading-in-Chunks

A strategy for reading rapidly is to look for the meaning in whole paragraphs and across paragraphs. This activity will help you practice reading-in-chunks, or taking in the meaning of a whole paragraph or group of words, by finding how the writer's focus shifts across paragraphs. The key words which signal these shifts are set out below. Fill in the correct paragraph numbers. In paragraphs 1 and 2, the writer's voice is expressed as "I." In what paragraph does the focus shift?

paragraph(s)	*focus*
1. _____	I
2. _____	our, we (people in the Western world)
3. _____	he says (drawing on material from an outside source, a book by Rifkin.)
4. _____	us (a transition paragraph)
5. _____	my

Using Context Clues

Some words, often those which are not key to the overall meaning, can be guessed by using clues in the immediate context. You should be able to understand the following words. Use the line provided to write a paraphrase of each.

guess the meaning

clues

1. para. 1
   I have <u>shed</u> its manufactured time

   I have taken time off . . .
   I have shed my city wardrobe (clothes)

   Notice the play on words:
   "to take off" means to take a vacation; Goodman uses the expression to mean taking off, or shedding a wristwatch.

   _____

2. para. 2
   <u>blueberry, raspberry, blackberry</u>

   they all are part of the world of seasons

   _____

3. para. 3
    <u>mussels, mackerel</u>

    at low tide I can harvest them; at high
    tide they swim into the cove

4. para. 8
    <u>icons</u>

    they are like clocks of temporal time;
    they began to rival churches in the city
    squares

5. para. 5
    <u>to strap time on</u>

    The meaning lies across paragraphs. Re-
    member the wristwatch Goodman shed
    at the beginning of her vacation? A wrist-
    watch is strapped on; it is held in place
    by a strap (or band).

Expressions with Time

The selection is filled with phrases and expressions which contain the word
"time." Many are listed below. Locate each in the selection. With a partner or
in a small group, discuss the meaning of each. Select those which are unfamiliar
and add them to your Personal Vocabulary–Building Notebook.

manufactured time	timelessness
to lose track of time	victory over time
timekeepers	timeframe
a time to	

Contrasts in Meaning

Goodman contrasts two ways of keeping track of time:

by numbers	by nature
(by the clock)	(by the seasons)

Find words and expressions in the article which pertain to each. Circle those
which are new to you. Enter them in your Personal Vocabulary–Building Notebook.

TALKING/WRITING ABOUT ———————————

1. With a partner or in a small group, discuss these expressions which are all related to time. Tell the others about expressions in your first language which are related or similar.

    Time is money.

    There is no time like the present.

    Time flies.

    Time waits for no one.

    Let's beat the clock.

    Ahead of /behind the times

    A time to reap and a time to sow

    The time of one's life

2. What book(s) do you think Ellen Goodman took along for pleasure reading on her vacation? Make a list of five selections. Compare your list with the others.

3. Write a composition in which you describe your own relationship to time:

    Do you live by the seasons or by the clock?

    Have you had a period in your life when you experienced a sense of timelessness?

    Has time ever stood still for you?

    Brainstorm the writing assignment before you start. Share your first draft with a partner. Give your partner feedback and get feedback on your own writing from your partner.

Letters: Obsolete Technology

A Note About . . .

Jack Smith is a noted columnist for a daily newspaper in Los Angeles. His readers think of him as their next door neighbor because he writes the way one good friend talks to another. His articles are about topics which are close to home. Sometimes, though, he takes on controversial issues, too; but his tone is always light and friendly.

BEFORE READING

To Think About:

1. At first, reading this article will seem like coming in after the program began since it contains readers' responses to something which appeared in a previous article by Smith. But once you realize this fact, you will be able to understand the discussion quite well.

2. You can easily guess from the title how the readers responded: They wrote

Vocabulary Preparation

Become familiar with these key expressions:

obsolete
obsoleted   no longer in use, outdated

state of the art   the latest, most up-to-date technology

To Look For:

1. Section 1: What were the issues in the earlier article that resulted in readers' complaints?

2. Section 2: What are the responses to that earlier discussion which Smith includes in this article?

3. Section 3: How does Smith react to his readers' letters? In the end, does he change his own viewpoint?

Now, read the entire selection without looking up words in the dictionary.

Letters: Obsolete Technology

By Jack Smith

1 READERS' complaints that our young people are helpless when thrown back on obsolete technology, such as the dial telephone and simple addition, have aroused a protest.

You may remember reading here about the fifth-grade pupil who wanted to call home from school but didn't know how to use the dial phone, and the ice cream parlor that had to close because the computerized cash register broke down.

These stories suggested that young people are almost wholly dependent on state of the art technology, and also that we older people are being obsoleted along with the machines of our era.

Perhaps it is the latter that hurts.

□

2 John A. Junot wants to know whether, if my car broke down, I would know how to ride a horse.

I might be willing to try. But the problem is—where could I ride one?

Junot suggests that I would either get the car repaired or replace it. That is what today's young engineers do when their computers break down, he points out.

In that respect I am as dependent on modern technology as the young. I have allowed myself to become wholly dependent on my computer, and when it breaks down I am like a man cast adrift at sea in a small boat.

"Cultures do not lose arts and skills," Junot argues. "They abandon them. Calculating by slide rule is in exactly the same class as archery, blacksmithing, sailing, hand-weaving and drawing. To the extent that those things are done, they are done by hobbyists, historians and cultural anthropologists and are preserved mainly by librarians."

Junot points out that certain ancient skills, such as archery and sailing, are themselves improved by modern technology. "Robin Hood probably couldn't shoot one of today's graphite/epoxy compound bows."

He says: "And so to that fifth-grader who didn't know how to dial a dial-type phone, you imply that the boy was somehow culturally deprived, and that it would 'come in handy' if he learned.

"I fail to see how. Rotary-dial phones are going the way of high-button shoes; they are uncommon now and doomed to extinction simply because you can't talk to computers with a rotary-type phone."

Junot points out that the first computers are already obsolete. I know what he means. I bought the first IBM Personal Computer on the market. Recently I blew what is known as the "mother card." It was replaced by a

106

more advanced clone card that is not perfectly compatible with my machine. I have had little but misery with it ever since.

Junot says it would have been impossible for the ice cream clerks to go on doing business, making their calculations by hand, when their computerized register failed.

"Well, before cash registers were invented, business *was* done that way. And employees stole because it was easy. Cash registers were invented precisely to keep employees honest, and to protect them from charges of dishonesty. . . ."

"Furthermore, computerized receipts are used for computing sales tax and the printouts for people buying on expense accounts. Are you suggesting that the kids give the businessman and the tax man numbers scribbled on the backs of paper sacks? The manager was probably only following the company policy when he closed the store. . . ."

Evidently, then, we have seen the end of mental calculations. Those fast-food computers even note the amount of money the customer pays and also the exact amount of change due. The clerk doesn't even have to figure out how much change is due from a $10 bill, nor does the customer, since he can assume that the computer doesn't err.

It's OK with me. I never was any good at arithmetic, anyway, and I'm glad I have lived long enough to see it obsoleted.

Meanwhile, Barbara Jones of Santa Barbara wonders how children can

ever learn how to tell time when all they see are digital watches.

And Sally Wade wonders, "How will tomorrow's adult (today's child) ever master a wrench, spigot, tap, screw or the like when the directions tell him/her to turn it 'clockwise' or 'counterclockwise' in this age of digital clocks?"

□

3   Why would tomorrow's adult ever have to use a wrench or a screwdriver?

Anyway, I think schoolroom clocks still have hands.

I will give the last word to Barbara L. Sigman of Simi Valley:

"I cannot let your article escape me without at least a murmur of protest. The 'young' are not all a bunch of mindless, albeit charming, beautiful and healthy people, as you imply. . . . Some of us read Shakespeare, Flaubert, and even Voltaire! Better yet, we can dial telephones and we can make change. And a few of us know a tiny bit about history, too."

Thank you, Ms. Sigman.

I'm glad to know that all is not lost.

AFTER THE FIRST READING ━━━━━━━━━━━━━

Which of the following are the central issues? You may check all, any number, or none. Be ready to explain your choices.

_____ Older people criticize young people because they only know how to use the latest technological inventions.

_____ Smith's readers are critical of his views of young people.

_____ When a technology becomes obsolete, it should be abandoned, or done away with.

Read the selection again. Then go on to the section, Building Reading Skills.

BUILDING READING SKILLS ━━━━━━━━━━━━

New and Old Technologies

Many new and old (state of the art and obsolete) technologies are mentioned in the article. Find as many as you can. List them in the correct categories:

Obsolete   *State of the Art*

What other technological inventions which are not mentioned can you add to these lists? For example: an icebox, a player piano, a compact disc player . . . .

Understanding the Views of the Letter-Writers

1. In Section 2: Smith reports what a reader named John A. Junot wrote to him. Smith uses various verbs to make it clear which are Junot's points and which are his own.

   For example: "Junot wants to know . . ."

   Find as many of these verbal expressions as you can. List them on the line below:

   _____

2. In addition, he includes the views expressed in other letters. Find the verbs used for quoting from Barbara Jones, Sally Wade, and Barbara Sigman. Write them on the line below:

   _____

Understanding Smith's View

1. In Section 1: How do you know that Smith's viewpoint represents older people?

    How old do you think Smith is?

    _____ under 50   _____ over 50

    Be ready to explain your answers.

2. In Section 2: Does Smith hold on to his original view? How does he show that he is at least considering Junot's arguments? What do these comments by Smith imply?
    a) I am as dependent on modern technology as the young.
    b) I know what he means . . .
    c) I never was any good at arithmetic.

3. In Section 3: Why does Smith give reader Barbara Sigman the last word? Explain your answer below.

    _____

    _____

    In the final line, what does Smith imply about his point of view on state of the art technology and young people?

TALKING/WRITING ABOUT ——————————

1. The article mentions a number of technological inventions. For example: telephones, computers, automobiles, digital watches, etc.

    In a group, share your views: What state of the art products of modern technology are important in your life? Make a list. Compare yours with the others'.

2. Jack Smith has invited his readers to write to him:
    *   of all the inventions of modern technology, which one would you be least willing to do without?
    *   on the other hand, what would you be most willing to give up?

    Write a letter to Smith. Be sure to give him the reasons for your choices.

Name Changes That Fracture Language

A Note About . . .

> S. B. Master doesn't usually write feature stories. In fact, her writing activities are generally within the business world. You can read about the author in the brief bio-information line which is at the bottom of page 114.

BEFORE READING ━━━━━━━━━━━━━

To Think About:

1. From the title and from knowing something about the author, can you guess what the article is about?

    _____ Name changes bring good luck.

    _____ Name changes go against the rules of language.

    _____ Corporate name changes, if done expertly, are good for business.

2. Read the first paragraph. In it, the author calls naming experts "phoneme scramblers" (*phonemes* are sounds in a language that have meaning). She says that they produce "computer-generated gibberish" (*gibberish* is meaningless language).

    Read the last paragraph. Do you think the author is against all name changes for business, or just some?

Vocabulary Preparation

Look for these expressions which all contain the word "computer."

computer-generated gibberish

computer-generated names

(a) computer-generated creation

Words and phrases with "computer" are contrasted with a number of expressions all borrowed from the vocabulary of hand sewing. By selecting these words, what point is the writer making? Use your English-English dictionary to check the meaning of any of the following that are unfamiliar.

bits and pieces

remnants

electronically stitched

patchwork

synthetic threads

To Look For:

1. The article contains many brief paragraphs. Some paragraphs only have one sentence. So you know it was intended to be read rapidly.

2. The author argues that names changes can "fracture language." As you read, look for the many examples she presents to prove his point.

3. She also presents some basic principles for good names. What are they?

Name Changes That Fracture Language

By S. B. Master

1 IN a misguided effort to liberate themselves from what management perceives as old, restrictive company names, many otherwise sensible corporate executives have run to phoneme scramblers, a breed of naming experts who seem to have given up on the language in favor of computer-generated gibberish.

2 Bits and pieces of words, remnants of sound, are electronically stitched together to form new "words."

3 The result? A rash of prominent American companies are sporting new patchwork names such as Allegis, Unisys, Navistar, Nynex and Trinova. Not since Lewis Carroll's "Jabberwocky" have we seen so much phoneme scrambling.

4 Often the scramblers get so caught up in their synthetic threads that they forget the basics: differentiation and pronounceability.

Name is Ambiguous

5 For example, while Primerica, American Can's new moniker, is not a total embarrassment like Unisys, its pronunciation (PRY-merica) is ambiguous and the "merica" suffix, although meaningful, is hackneyed.

6 There are already many federally registered corporations or trademarks with names ending in "merica" (Homerica, Comerica, Agrimerica) and others beginning with "Ameri" (Ameritech, Amerifirst, etc.). So it will be very difficult and costly to make Primerica stand out.

7 Coining words is definitely not the same as minting money. Names such as Exxon and Abex may be good or bad. But one thing is certain: They will require many promotional dollars to establish.

8 With enough time and money, any meaningless and fairly pronounceable combination of letters can be made a part of the language.

9 But that's an expensive way to go. A new word will always need more introductory promotion than a real word already charged with meaning.

10 Our experience both nationally and internationally proves that people respond most positively to names that they can use easily, understand quickly and feel good *about*.

11 Real words, with the emotional and psychological associations they carry, generally do a better job of accomplishing these objectives. It isn't easy for people to get a warm feeling from abstract and meaningless computer-generated names.

12 Dangers abound in phoneme scrambling. Sometimes a computer-made creation turns out, embarrassingly enough, to be an obscure real word.

13 When Houston Natu-

ral Gas and Inter-North merged last year, the marriage resulted in the awkward moniker HNG/InterNorth. Management agreed to rename the company (something coined, something related to energy and high tech).

14   It very nearly ended up with Enteron Corp. until it learned from a very amused investment community that the word *enteron* is the medical term for the alimentary canal, an organ that functions both in digestion and the elimination of waste. Back to the minting machine.

15   Another naming mistake, almost as common and also resulting in a meaningless miasma, is the Alphabet Soup Solution.

16   In the age of mergers and acquisitions, many good corporate names have been replaced by a string of letters. It works with RAC, IBM and GE. Why not then PPG or MBPXL?

17   The answer is obvious. Only companies with a long history of very high visibility can get away with shorthand initials.

Beware of Blunders

18   Running to the alphabet is often the easiest way out—and a sure sign of the naming expert's fatigue. For every AT&T or GE there are hundreds of SMCs, DPFs, GAFs and—most tragic of all—USXs

that have chosen alphabetical anonymity.

19   The Nearsighted Name also is a hazard. Always keep an eye to the future. With too specific a name, you can fence yourself into a single market, product or service and create problems for future diversification.

20   Beware especially of geographically limiting names. Allegheny Airlines had a geographically nearsighted name. Its current name, USAir, immediately changed the public perception, communicating its nationwide service.

21   Names often build up tremendous equity. If a new name won't do a better job of achieving your objectives, keep the old one and revitalize it with

a fresh, new visual treatment.

22   For example, new corporate color, judiciously selected typography, a revised logo and a systematic approach to graphics can be powerful—and instant—communicators of corporate strategy.

23   Lastly, beware of the Dirty Word blunder. Even if you think that your market is limited for the moment to the English speaking world, don't forget the large and growing non-English-speaking population in the United States.

24   Also remember that today's marketplace is becoming more and more global. Forward-thinking management should anticipate expansion.

25   Names, therefore, should be checked with the major languages of the world so that awkward homonyms can be avoided.

26   Chevy Nova, for example, means "no go" in Spanish, and Colgate means "hang yourself" when given the Spanish pronunciation, col-gah-tay.

27   While it's great fun to call attention to the current lunacy in naming that seems to be sweeping corporate America, it should be remembered that naming is a serious business.

28   In these days of intensified competition the right name can be an enormous advantage in the marketplace.

S. B. Master is in charge of the corporate naming division of Landor Associates, San Francisco, California.

AFTER THE FIRST READING ━━━━━━━━━

Chose only *one*.

1.   The writer is critical of:

     _____ sensible corporate executives

     _____ all naming experts

     _____ some naming experts

2.   Important basic principles for changes are that the name can be (choose *two*):

     _____ advertised   _____ pronounced   _____ differentiated (understood)

Read the selection again. Then go on to the section, Building Reading Skills.

BUILDING READING SKILLS ────────

Finding The Examples

You were correct when you checked "Pronounceability" and "Differentiation" as the writer's two principles for a good name change. The article gives many examples of name changes that do not follow these basic principles. Find as many as you can. You decide if each is an example of a *pronounciation problem* or a *meaning problem.*

pronunciation problems

example: in paragraph

_____

_____

meaning problems

example: in paragraph

_____

_____

Understanding Word Meanings from Context

You can understand the meaning of some unfamiliar words by using clues in the immediate context.

guess the meaning

1. para. 5
   Primerica, American Can's new <u>mon-iker</u>.

2. para. 13
   . . . an awkward <u>moniker</u>

3. para. 5
   The suffix "-merica" although meaningful is <u>hackneyed</u>

clues

1. The new name is "Primerica." The topic is new names. A <u>moniker</u> is a

   _____

2. the topic is still "names"

   _____

   (it's used in informal language)

3. There are already many . . . with names ending in "-merica," so <u>hack-neyed</u> =

   _____

4. para. 5
    Primerica, its pronunciation (Prymer-ica) is <u>ambiguous</u>

4. Primerica could also be pronounced, PREmerica. So, <u>ambiguous</u> =

    _____

    a) unclear meaning because of two possibilities;
    b) false meaning

5. para. 21
    names build up tremendous <u>equity</u>

5. Keep the old one. Revitalize it. So, <u>equity</u>

    = _____

    a) service
    b) value

Creating New Words

1. In paragraph 7:
    "Coining words is not the same as minting money."

    a) Who *mints* money? to mint = to manufacture or make coins

        _____

    b) Who *coins* new words? to coin = to create or make up

        _____

    c) Why are the two not the same?

        _____

2. American English is particularly noted for adopting newly coined words. Some come from the world of business and advertising, some from popular music, some from sports.

    A few examples are given below. Do you know all of them? Try to add to the list.

    Xerox   Kodak   Coke   rock-n-roll

    _____

    _____

    _____

    _____

TALKING/WRITING ABOUT

1. What new, useful words have you entered into your Personal Vocabulary–Building Notebook that you found in "Name Changes?"

2. With a partner: choose roles, one person is the sensible corporate executive, a president of a company that is contemplating a corporate name change. The other person is S. B. Master of Landor Associates, San Francisco, a firm that specializes in enhancing corporate images.

   You must decide on the nature of your business, its size, location, chief markets, competition, . . .

   The corporate executive calls Ms. Master to find out more about the services her company offers. Before calling, make an outline of the information you are seeking. For example: the fees, the guarantees of success, the scope of the services, charges for extra services, references from other clients . . .

3. Use the ideas that were generated by you and your partner in the role-play to write either a) or b) as a follow-up to the telephone call.

   a) The corporate executive writes a letter to Ms. Master telling her that (you complete the scenario)

   _____

   b) As a follow-up to the inquiry from the corporate executive, Ms. Master writes a letter restating the information she gave over the telephone. She really wants to get this account (you complete the scenario)

   _____

Aggressiveness Doesn't Always Work in Business

A Note About . . .

> The author, an executive with a public relations firm, wrote this feature story for a general audience of readers. In many ways, however, it is similar to a case-study, a form of writing widely used in management and business. Look back at Selection 3 in Unit Two to see an example of a mini case study.

BEFORE READING ━━━━━━━━━━━━━━━━━━━━━━

To Think About:

1. Why is the title a *paradox*? (A paradox is a statement which seems contradictory.)

2. What information does the subtitle give about the subject of the article?

3. Read paragraph 1. *sine qua non* (Latin) = something which is essential.

   Even if you don't recognize the names of these heroes in the business world, you can understand that the article will present a case which (select one):

   _____ goes against popular wisdom

   _____ supports aggressiveness in business

   _____ praises the American style of management

Vocabulary Preparation

As you read the article, look for these word groups.

a classic case	an example that best and uniquely illustrates a point
a brute-force approach	all muscles and no brains
a market winner	a product that sells well
a critical flaw	a crucial mistake
an elegant concept	an economical, novel idea
a tempting contrast	the difference between Sony and JVC's terms made JVC very attractive
a take-it-or-leave-it approach	accept our terms or we will quit the discussion

To Look For:

1. What are the important companies in this classic case?

2. What point of view does the case study illustrate?

3. Where does the case study begin? Mark the paragraph number.

Aggressiveness Doesn't Always Work in Business

Development of 2 VCR Systems Is a Classic Case

By John M. Ketteringham

1 ASK Lee Iacocca or Ron Perelman, Carl C. Icahn or George Steinbrenner. They'll assure you that aggressiveness is the *sine qua non* of business today. To conquer a market as swiftly and as uncompromisingly as possible is an imperative that permeates the American style of management.

2 In researching a series of extraordinary commercial successes that have transformed people's lives in the last two decades, my associates and I found little support for such a brute-force approach as it applies to dramatically new commercial concepts.

3 In repeated instances, we saw that aggression and haste were negative factors — elements more likely to threaten an exceptional new idea than to advance it.

4 Indeed, in tapping international sources and investment, in acquisitions and in the recruiting of executive leaders, aggressiveness is necessary. But in the realm of creativity, kid gloves work better than boxing gloves.

5 There was no better example of this paradox than in the development of the videocassette recorder, a 20-year dream of consumer electronics companies throughout the world that finally came to pass in Japan between 1971 and 1976.

6 The final competitors in the effort to create a VCR technology that was simple, small and inexpensive enough for home use by regular TV-watching consumers were two companies with drastically different philosophies, Sony Corp. and Victor Co. of Japan, otherwise known as JVC.

'Polite, Gentle, Understanding'

7 In an interview, a highly placed Sony manager expressed that company's philosophy: "It's a Sony policy that we should be the leader from the very beginning, from technology to market share. We should always advance the product ahead of everyone else. We should dominate the market from beginning to end."

8 Compare this to a comment by Shizuo Takano, known as "the father of VHS (Video Home System)," in discussing JVC's approach to videocassette recorder development: "Our basic policy was to spread the information as well as to spread the technology and the format.

9 The market is large enough to hold everybody. So we don't have to worry about that. Japan does not have to monopolize the video market. One single company does not have to monopolize the whole profit."

10   Even more dramatic is a philosophy expressed by former JVC President Kokichi Matsuno on the day he assumed his firm's leadership in 1975.

11   "The most important value for the people in our company," Matsuno told his assembled managers, "is that you should be very polite and gentle . . . a JVC person should be one who can understand what your business partner is thinking."

12   What Takano and Matsuno both expressed was not just a moral lesson, but an approach to blending opportunity with creativity in the business world.

13   Let's look at what happened in the competition between Sony and JVC. The clear divergence in their outlooks began in 1971.

14   That year, the two companies joined forces with Matsushita Electric and created a single set of technical standards to govern development of a videotape recorder that used a ¾-inch-wide magnetic tape.

15   That collaboration of Sony, JVC and Matsushita—Japan's largest consumer electronics company—was extraordinary because they shared engineers, plans, patents—the works.

16   In the end, however, it was Sony's product that emerged from this joint research effort as the market winner. Moving aggressively into the broadcast, corporate and institutional markets, Sony became dominant in ¾-inch videotape recorders.

17   For the leaders of the VCR research effort at JVC—Takano and a scholarly, brilliant cohort named Yuma Shiraishi—Sony's ¾-inch videotape recorder victory had profound implications.

18   The company had been losing battles to Sony for a long time, and for JVC senior management it was the last straw. The firm in 1971 canceled almost all its support for the VCR research program.

19   For Takano and Shiraishi, the defeat was more personal, because they had been stymied once again in their quest to fulfill a dream they harbored for more than 15 years.

20   It was a dream they had inherited from their beloved teacher, Kenjiro Takayanagi, the "godfather" of video at JVC, a man who in 1926 created television in Japan. For Takayanagi's sake, these two determined engineers had to press on—with JVC's official support or without it.

21   Takano and Shiraishi saw that both Sony and JVC had failed to invent the thing they wanted to invent—a VCR simple enough for everybody. The next stop in VCR evolution would be to a ½-inch tape width.

22   Sony was moving to that research stage based on its ¾-inch product success. But the view of Takano and Shiraishi was more insightful. They decided that, regardless of sales, all previous videotape machines were fundamentally flawed—because none had made the leap to the consumer market.

23   To catch up to Sony, which was moving quickly from its ¾-inch product to a ½-inch variation, JVC dropped out of the race and headed back to the starting line. "Looking back on all the failures, we decided to start out from scratch," Takano said. "All the work of the past was forgotten."

24 In halting the forward rush, Shiraishi and a small team of VCR research survivors perceived a number of critical flaws in the existing technology. People would not embrace a VCR, for instance, that had only one hour of tape in its cassette—even if the cassette was cunningly small.

25 The reason was simple: one hour wasn't long enough to record a feature-length movie. Other manufacturers would not embrace a one-hour VCR tape. Likewise, manufacturers would not welcome a VCR format that was difficult to build. Takano, more than Shiraishi and more than Sony, realized that the market for the first consumer VCR would not be consumers at all. It would be other manufacturers.

Network of Engineers

26 Hence, while Shiraishi and his team were devising a simple and nearly unbreakable tape machine that would satisfy consumers with at least two hours of playing time, Takano was busy informing and politicking through a network of engineers in all of Japan's major consumer electronics companies.

27 Repeatedly, Takano broke the secrecy of JVC research. Politely, gently, he built alliances among the companies JVC would need when VHS finally reached the market.

28 Blending technology, self-examination and politics, Shiraishi and Takano created the concept of the VHS format.

29 They carried out what my associates and I have come to call the "elegant concept," an idea expressed early in this century by Thomas A. Edison when he stated the essence of successful invention.

30 Even before you begin to build, he said, "all parts of the system must be constructed with reference to all other parts. . . . The failure of one part to cooperate properly with the other parts disorganizes the whole and renders it inoperative for the purpose intended."

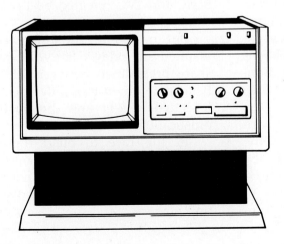

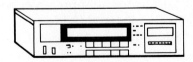

31   When, in mid-1974, Sony completed its prototype for the Betamax VCR, the first consumer VCR in history, the company tried to interest two of the world's largest TV manufacturers, first RCA in America, then Matsushita in Japan.

Flaws Unseen by Early Consumers

32   But there were flaws in Betamax, flaws unseen by the early consumers who rushed to buy this delightful new gadget. But these flaws were foreseen by Shiraishi and Takano.

33   They were flaws noticed by most of the manufacturers, including RCA and Matsushita. They were flaws that Sony refused to fix because Sony was in a hurry to reach the market with the first and the smallest VCR.

34   Betamax was flawed by manufacturing difficulties and by Sony's diplomatic failures. Sony executives had failed to discuss the new technology with other companies as they were developing it.

35   Most critically, Betamax was flawed by a cassette that provided consumers only one hour of playing time. By mid-1976, a year after Sony had introduced Betamax, these problems were manifest in the marketplace. Sony's sales were unimpressive, less than 200,000 units worldwide.

36   JVC came out 18 months later with the VHS, and its product was—in the words of Konosuke Matsushita, the grand old man of Japanese electronics—"something very nice."

37   Typically, JVC's first product introductions were neither for press nor public. They were presentations for other manufacturers. The statement that the polite but crafty Takano always made at these presentations was this: "Well, JVC has . . . come up with the prototype, but I am sure everyone else in this room has also developed some sort of prototype by now.

38   I don't really care which company's equipment or format we go for, but let's go for the best system we are all working on."

39   This air of HVC humility, which combined the company's traditional diffidence with Takano's cleverness, was in striking contrast to Sony's take-it-or-leave-it attitude with the Beta format.

40   Not insignificantly, JVC's licensing terms for VHS were also a tempting contrast, both to Beta licensing terms and to the cost for other companies of continuing to seek their own ½-inch VCR format.

41   Patience, persistence, politeness truly won out in the "race" to dominate the VCR market. Both companies, Sony and JVC, created beautiful machines.

42   But in the end, the difference that resulted in today's 80%-20% market share breakdown between VHS and Beta came down to a difference in intellectual insight and diplomatic sophistication.

43   In the race to build the better mousetrap, Sony courted mice. But Yuma Shiraishi *understood* mice; and Shizuo Takano gently seduced mousetrap makers.

AFTER THE FIRST READING ━━━━━━━━━━━━

1. What companies were originally involved in developing the VCR?

    _____   _____   _____

2. Is the writer in favor of aggressiveness or "an air of humility" in the business world?

    _____

3. The case study begins in paragraph ____. The first words are "Let's look at what happened . . ."

Read the selection again. Then, go on to the section Building Reading Skills.

BUILDING READING SKILLS ━━━━━━━━━━

Finding Key Terms

This case study illustrates two approaches in the business/management world. In many ways, the approaches apply to all areas of human activity. The author uses two contrasting terms, *kid gloves* and *boxing gloves* to illustrate the approaches.

Find as many words and phrases in the article as you can which fit under either one of these terms. Compare your lists with your partner's.

kid gloves   *boxing gloves*

Vocabulary Extension

Review your understanding of the noun phrases you first met in the section, Vocabulary Preparation, by matching the items in columns A and B correctly.

	A.		*B.*
1.	The development of the VCR was	____	a brute-force approach
2.	One critical flaw	____	a tempting contrast
3.	Commercial success does not involve	____	aggressiveness in the business world
4.	New inventions, according to Thomas Edison, should be	____	a market winner

5. The VCR has been   _____ a classic case

6. Faced with a choice, the JVC terms   _____ involved playing time
   were

7. A take-it-or-leave-it attitude indicates   _____ elegant concepts

Close Reading

You have been asked to give a two minute oral summary of this case study at a seminar you are attending on managerial strategies. The task requires close reading, finding the details that illustrate main ideas.

Make notes to use for a brief oral report on the three critical flaws in the Sony approach to developing a VCR system. Contrast it with the JVC approach. An outline is provided.

1. The time factor

2. The manufacturing factor

3. The political factor

Well-known Expressions:

The article contains a number of expressions and figures of speech often used in American English. In each case, the meaning of the phrase is not literal, it is figurative. You should recognize most of them.

Scan the article again to locate the paragraphs which contain the following phrases. Use an English-English dictionary to check for the meaning of any which are unclear. Or, you may need to consult your teacher or a native-speaker. Which have you decided to enter into your Personal Vocabulary-Building Notebook? Be ready to tell your partner or your group.

Paragraph

1. *Kid gloves* work better than *boxing gloves*.   _____

2. For JVC management, it was *the last straw*.   _____

3. JVC . . . headed back *to the starting line*.   _____

4. We decided to start *from scratch*.   _____

5. It was a race to build a *better mousetrap*.   _____

TALKING/WRITING ABOUT ─────────

1. In a group, discuss this main issue:
   According to the author, aggressiveness didn't work in the Sony vs. JVC case. But does it work in other instances, both in and out of the business world? For example, in family life, in personal relationships, in the workplace, in school? What are your ideas on kid gloves vs. boxing gloves?

2. Did you write a mini case study after reading "Characteristics of the Organizational Behavior Field" in Unit Two? If not, now that you have read "Aggressiveness in Business . . ." you may have ideas about applying the case study writing technique to a situation with which you have first-hand experience.

   Remember, your report could be from the point-of-view of a consumer of goods and products as well as that of a producer of products, such as VCR systems.

   For example: Interview users of the two VCR systems described in the article. Use the information in the article as your source for asking questions. Then, use the mini case study as a model for writing your findings.

   Be sure to get feedback on your writing from others in the group.

The Paradox of Power and The Way Beyond Babel

A Note About . . .

Have you ever made a long-distance telephone call in the United States? If you have, the chances are you heard the operator say: "Thank you for using AT&T." AT&T is a corporate name that is so well-known that the letters alone have meaning. They are pronounced separately as "ey t and t." If you don't know what the letters stand for, ask your teacher or someone who makes many long-distance telephone calls.

BEFORE READING

To Think About:

1. The skillful reader knows that both ads on pages 127 and 129 present the point of view of the advertiser, a multinational communications corporation. How does the reader know this?

   Both ads appeared in newspapers and magazines throughout North America within the same year.

2. Read the titles:

   "The Paradox of Power": Can you guess what the message will be? Does the illustration offer any clues? What does it show?

   "The Way Beyond Babel": Can you guess what the message will be? Does the drawing offer any clues? What does it show?

Vocabulary Preparation

Check your understanding of these key terms before reading.

1. In "The Paradox of Power":

paradox	from your previous reading, you can guess that the ad presents a *paradoxical* situation about power
potential	a capability which is not yet functioning
to cope with	to manage or succeed
rigid	difficult or unbending
breakthrough	a major achievement

Issues of the Information Age:

The paradox of power.

© 1987 AT&T

The Information Age, for all its potential, has brought with it a new kind of problem. Often, the machines that contribute so much to the flood of information do little to help most of us cope with it. They are difficult to use, rigid in their demands, almost arrogant in their inability to work with any but their own kind. They are the muscle-bound tools of specialists.

In our view, the problem is not that the machines are too powerful for the rest of us. They are not powerful enough.

This is the paradox of power: the more powerful the machine, the less power it exerts over the person using it. We define a more powerful machine as one that is more capable of bending to the will of humans, rather than having humans bend to its will. The definition is deeply ingrained in AT&T. The telephone is such a powerful device precisely because it demands so little of its user.

AT&T foresees the day when the Information Age will become universal. People everywhere will participate in a worldwide Telecommunity. They will be able to handle information in any form—conversation, data, images, text—as easily as they now make a phone call.

That day is coming closer. One example: scientists at AT&T Bell Laboratories are developing "associative" memories for computers, further enabling the machines to work with incomplete, imprecise, or even contradictory information. That's perfectly natural for a human. What makes it a breakthrough is that these computers won't ask you to be anything else.

Telecommunity is our goal. Technology is our means.™

We are committed to leading the way.

AT&T

2.   In "The Way Beyond Babel":

(the Tower of) **babel**	a figurative phrase (from the Bible, Book of Genesis) which implies that people all speak different languages and so cannot communicate with each other
track gauge	the measure of distance between railroad tracks
proprietary	privately owned
de facto	(Latin) something existing in reality, though not in law
incompatibility	incapable of working together

To Look For:

1.   Look for the central message: the illustrations seem to be advertising computers and railroads. Are these the machines which AT&T sells?

2.   Do both ads state the same message? Or, do they deal with different issues of the information age?

Issues of the Information Age:

The way beyond Babel.

Imagine trying to build a railroad system if every locomotive manufacturer used a different track gauge. Every local stretch of railroad had its own code of signals. And in order to ride a train, you needed to know the gauges and the signals and the switching procedures and the route and the conductor's odd pronunciation of the station names.

The business of moving and managing information is in a similar state today. Machines can't always talk to each other. Proprietary systems and networks abound, with suppliers often jockeying to make theirs the <u>de facto</u> standard. The enormous potential of the Information Age is being dissipated by incompatibility.

The solution, as we see it, is common standards which would allow electronic systems in one or many locations to work together. People will be informed and in control, while the systems exchange, process, and act on information automatically.

AT&T is working with national, international, and industry-wide organizations to set up comprehensive, international standards to be shared by everyone who uses and provides information technology. We think it's time for everyone in our industry to commit to developing firm, far-reaching standards. The goal: to provide our customers with maximum flexibility and utility. Then, they can decide how and with whom to work.

We foresee a time when the promise of the Information Age will be realized. People will participate in a worldwide Telecommunity through a vast, global network of networks, the merging of communications and computers. They'll be able to handle information in any form—conversation, data, images, text—as easily as they make a phone call today.

The science is here now. The technology is coming along rapidly. But only with compatibility will the barriers to Telecommunity recede.

<u>Telecommunity is our goal. Technology is our means.</u>

We're committed to leading the way.

AT&T

AFTER THE FIRST READING ━━━━━━━

1. With what machine of the information age is AT&T primarily concerned?

   _____

2. Which view do you support?
   a) Both ads say the same thing
   b) Both ads make comments about the information age, but they focus on different aspects

If you are not sure of the answer, read both selections again. Then, go on to the section Building Reading Skills.

BUILDING READING SKILLS ━━━━━━━

Locating Essential Elements I (the *sine qua non*)

In "The Paradox of Power": Machines, we are told, do little to help us cope with the flood of information in our lives because they are:

1) _____
2) _____
3) _____
4) _____

A more powerful machine is capable of:

5) _____

Using Your Background Information I

You have already read about the information issue which "The Paradox of Power" describes.

Look back at Selection 3 in this Unit. Find the paragraph in which Jack Smith ("Letters: Obsolete Technology") described the difficulties he had with computer incompatibility.

Do you think Smith would agree or disagree with the AT&T ad? Why? Write your answer below:

_____

Locating Essential Elements II (the *sine qua non*)

In "The Way Beyond Babel": The ad uses the railroad figuratively to suggest the problems in new technologies brought about by the incompatibility of different systems.

Actually, 100 years ago the railroads had the problem of standard track gauges which the illustration shows.

Why is the current state of moving and manufacturing information similar to that of the railroads' problem? Find the key phrases which answer that question by completing the lines below:

1. Machines _____

2. Proprietary _____

3. Suppliers _____

What is the solution outlined in paragraphs 3, 4? Explain it in your own words:

_____

Using Your Background Information II

In "The Way Beyond Babel": You have already read about the information age issue which the AT&T ad suggests. Look back at Selection 5 in this Unit, "Aggressiveness Doesn't Always Work in Business." Scan to find the paragraphs which describe the development of VCR systems. What did that industry do to achieve compatible systems?

What do you think Kenjiro Takayanagi (the "godfather" of video) would say about this AT&T ad? Write a brief summary of your opinions:

TALKING/WRITING ABOUT _____

1. In a group, compare the two ads. Do you believe they present:

    _____ the same issue   _____ different issues   _____ related issues

    Which one focuses on an issue which concerns the consumers of information age machines?

    Which ad focuses on an issue which concerns the producers of information age machines?

    Give evidence for your opinions.

2. Write a Letter To The Editor of the newspaper which published these AT&T ads (you select the name of the paper): Take a position regarding these ads.

    Do you believe they mislead readers? Do you believe they were effective in conveying information to the public? Do you believe the newspaper should publish more advertising from large corporations which contain messages which go beyond selling their product? (These ads are called "institutional advertising" or "public service advertisements.")

    In brainstorming the writing assignment, try to find other ads in newspapers of a similar type. Show them to your writing partners.

READING POPULAR SCIENCE

UNIT INTRODUCTION

READING POPULAR SCIENCE FOR ADDITIONAL INFORMATION ━━━━━━━━━━━

The topics in Unit Four will be familiar to you from your previous reading, particularly of selections from introductory textbooks in Unit Two. Reading about science, as in all subject areas, becomes easier and more satisfying when you have begun to acquire a background of basic information. As you read the selections in Unit Four, you will realize how much you have already learned.

Writing for non-scientists, called "popular science writing," appears in newspaper feature sections, magazines of all kinds, and non-fiction books. There are a number of magazines devoted entirely to popular science subjects. You can expect that, unlike scientific papers published in professional journals, popular science is written to hold your attention.

Writing popular science requires considerable scientific background along with a talent for making the material interesting. Unit Four selections are by some of the best people in the business. A few of them, for example Jared Diamond and Stephen Jay Gould, are working scientists who also write about their specialization for non-scientists. Both Isaac Asimov and Bettyann Kevles are prize-winning science writers.

It's Up To Us in a Time of Technology

A Note About . . .

Bettyann Kevles writes a syndicated column which appears in hundreds of newspapers. With a background in professional writing, she has made science her special area. Noted as a topnotch science writer, her articles and non-fiction books have won prizes.

BEFORE READING

To Think About:

1. Read the title. Which statement below does it seem to imply (suggest without clearly stating)?
    *   Society as a whole should decide what technologies are developed.
    *   Society as a whole should decide what technologies are not developed.
    *   The development of any technology should be avoided because it can cause destruction.

2. Read paragraph 1:
    The story of the wheel will be used to show that:
    *   The human race naturally develops new technologies.
    *   The development of technology is tied to the nature of the civilization in which it is found.
    *   All technologies develop in all societies in the same way.

Vocabulary Preparation

Become familiar with these words and expressions:

dead end	something which does not have the capability of growing or developing
a pulley	all are technologies derived from one of the first human inventions—the
a wheeled cart	wheel
a wheelbarrow	
a water wheel	
wheeled vehicles	

To Look For:

1. Along with the wheel, other significant technological inventions are discussed. What are they?

2. The writer makes a moral, ethical point about technology. What is it?

It's Up to Us in a Time of Technology

by Bettyann Kevles

1   The impetus to create new devices, elaborating upon what went before until a whole new level of technology is achieved, is not inherent in human nature. The history of civilizations is full of technological dead ends. What was the goal of one culture became the beginning of a whole stream of development in another. Take the wheel.

2   We don't know who invented it first. It may have been a potter, or it may have been a farmer eager to find a better way to transport a load. We do know that in the West, once noticed, wheels were paired and put on wheelbarrows, doubled again and attached to carts, and lined up with ropes to make them into simple machines—pulleys.

3   The great Mayan civilization in Mexico and Central America flourished at about the same time that Christianity was taking root in the Middle East and Europe. The Mayas were great architects who built large temple-cities without, it seems, the benefit of pulleys or wheeled carts. Yet they knew about the wheel, as miniature wheeled vehicles that look like toys have been found in their ruins. The mystery is why, if they knew enough to put them on toys, did they never develop wheels for work-saving devices?

□

4   Or what about the mechanical clock? Historian David Landes traces the first mechanical clock to 11th-Century China. Planned by Su Sung, a diplomat and amateur scientist, it was first made of wood, then reconstructed in bronze. This enormous clock occupied a 40-foot tower and reproduced the movements of the sun, the moon and selected stars. An assemblage of rings represented the paths of these heavenly bodies as they rotated on an axis tilted toward the horizon. These were driven by a pair of vertical transmission shafts, one of which bore enormous wheels that carried little figures that revolved with the wheel and shaft to show the hours and quarter hours. The whole machine was powered by a water wheel.

5   This great clock worked for several years until invaders carried part of it away. Most of the mechanism broke or wore down in the next few years and no one knew enough about it to build another. Not until the arrival of Christian missionaries 500 years later did the Chinese see a mechanical clock again. And when they did they admired and fussed over them, but made no attempt to copy or improve upon their workings.

6   The Chinese, in fact, had discovered a host of useful technologies, including movable type and gunpowder. Yet, like the mechanical clock, they saw these as ends in themselves, not as the first steps toward a printing press as in the case of type, powerful

weapons as in the case of gunpowder, or a continuing preoccupation with precision in the measurement of time in the case of the clock.

7 We do not know as much about the Mayan civilization, whose written language we are still deciphering, as we do about the Chinese, whose records are excellent and whose civilization has been continuous from antiquity through the present. What we know about the Mayas is that they were agricultural, living largely off maize, and devoted most of their spare time to a religion that focused on astronomy and a complicated (and exceedingly accurate) calendar. What we do know suggests that it was a civilization in which labor was cheap and time plentiful enough so that there was no impetus to devise ways to make labor more economical. They did not need wheeled vehicles or machinery.

8 The mechanical clock that Su Sung developed used a water wheel to power it and, according to Landes, was probably more accurate than the relatively clumsy mechanical clocks

that the Jesuits brought to China in their attempt to dazzle the Chinese with the accomplishments of Christendom. But, unlike the by-then-forgotten great water-powered clock, these were portable with fanciful moving figurines. They dazzled the courtiers, but not enough to inspire imitation. They could as easily have been admiring works of art as instruments to measure time.

□

9 This is, Landes explains, because it is not "natural" to human beings to want to know the precise time. The obsession with time as something that can be measured, and thus paid for in the sense of labor per unit of time, is what distinguishes the West from all other civilizations. It is what, he argues convincingly, compelled us to ever more technological ingenuity as we broke time down into smaller and more accurate units.

10 Inventions like the wheel and the mechanical clock do not carry within themselves the seeds of future tech-

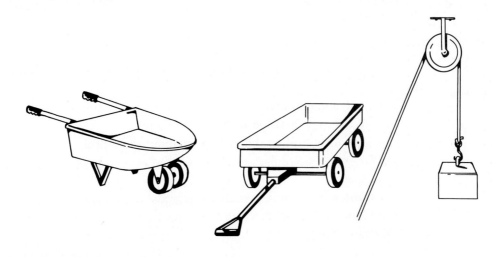

nological innovation. They are used by societies as the societies see fit. All inventions are not genii in a Pandora's box, that once released, have destinies of their own. Whether we can control the momentum of our own society is a complex moral, political and economic problem. But we dodge responsibility when we blame technology— be it nuclear, laser or biological—rather than the people who accept it without hesitation.

AFTER THE FIRST READING

Check all that are mentioned.

1. The inventions discussed include:

    _____ the wheel   _____ the mechanical clock   _____ movable type

    _____ gun powder   _____ the calendar

2. The writer's view is that:

    _____ technology can be directed by people

    _____ technology always controls people

Read the selection again. Then, go on to the section Building Reading Skills.

BUILDING READING SKILLS

Understanding Main Ideas

1. Which statements best rephrase the writer's main ideas? Discuss your answers with a partner:
    a) Some cultures are uninterested in technological developments.
    b) Human beings do not have an inherent drive to elaborate upon existing developments.
    c) One culture may adopt an invention which another culture leaves unfinished.

2. Choose one. The discussion of the wheel was included to make the point that:
    a) The same invention was put to different uses in different cultures.
    b) Only Western civilization really needed wheels.
    c) The Mayan civilization did not know about the wheel.

3. Choose one. The discussion of the mechanical clock was included to make the point that:
    a) The Chinese saw these inventions as ends in themselves.
    b) The Chinese did not have the materials available to further develop these inventions.

c) The Jesuits brought clocks that were more accurate than the early Chinese mechanical clock.

Understanding the Examples

According to Kevles, different civilizations make different adaptations to technological inventions. Summarize the facts presented in the article by writing a paragraph about the two civilizations she mentions.

Take the wheel and the mechanical clock, how did each of these civilizations adapt to them?

The Mayan civilization:

The Chinese civilization:

TALKING/WRITING ABOUT ────────────

1. In a group, discuss these questions:

    Where do science writers get their material? Who did Kevles interview for the ideas in this article? If you wanted to read more about Landes' hypotheses, where could you find his writing?

2. Landes said: "Keeping precise time is not natural." Yet, the physical world around us is tied to time. How could we think about distances in space without the idea of time? As the first human civilization with the capability of leaving this planet, where could we go without being able to keep precise time?

3. Compare a historian's view of time with Ellen Goodman's view by looking back at Selection 2 in Unit Three. If Goodman interviewed Landes, what would she ask him? What aspect of his ideas would fascinate her? What ideas would she use from the interview to write about?

In your group, or with a partner, role-play a Landes/Goodman interview. Use the ideas that come out of the interview as the basis for writing an article about the length of an Ellen Goodman column.

The Digital Age

A Note About . . .

Warren Kalbacker has written articles for many popular science magazines. A skillful reporter, he knows how to seek out top authorities to answer his questions. To write this article, he contacted "some of the science-fiction boys."

BEFORE READING

To Think About:

1. Read the title: What relationship does "digital age" have to AT&T's "information age?"

2. Read paragraph 1:
   - Do you experience time in a digital way, or in a spatial way? What is the difference?
   - "Some children even learn to tell time on them." What did Jack Smith and some of his readers think about children who don't learn to tell time with spatial clocks? (Scan Selection 3, Unit 3.)
   - What is the difference between experiencing time "like sand in an hourglass" or as "discrete and discontinuous?"

Vocabulary Preparation

Which of the following are new words for you? Which ones will you enter in your Personal Vocabulary-Building Notebook?

digital	a unit of measurement, a digit
discrete	something with individual parts
discontinuous	- - - - a discontinuous line
drudgery	hard, menial work
distortion–free	without interference
harbinger	it goes before and makes known what is approaching
hybrid	a mixture of types

To Look For:

The author is concerned about one central question. But there is a fairly long introduction and build–up to the central question.

- What is the question?
- Where does it occur?

The Digital Age

by Warren Kalbacker

1 I have a fond memory of a clock that hung in one of my elementary school classrooms during the 1950s, in the days when computer power was measured in the number of man-centuries of accountant time the machines would save. Looking back now I can see that clock was a harbinger of the digital age we are now entering. The clock was a hybrid. It had a face like all clocks of the day, but instead of gliding smoothly and continuously, its hands paused at each mark on the circular face and then deliberately leaped to the next mark with a regular rhythm, as though time did not exist in the interval. Not surprisingly, the clock was made by that digital giant, IBM. By now we have become accustomed to experiencing time in a digital way. Digital clocks and watches are everywhere; some children even learn to tell time on them. In the predigital era, we thought of time as flowing uninterruptedly, like sand in an hourglass. Minutes and seconds were inexact, and "now" was impossible to pin down. The hands of a clock moved through space. But digitized time is changing all that. Computer technology treats time like any other information to be processed: each unit of time is broken into a theoretically endless series of zeros and ones. Digital seconds or minutes are discrete, and like the hybrid clock of my youth, they are also discontinuous.

2 In the old days, when we looked at our watches and saw we had 10 minutes to get somewhere, we saw those 10 minutes as a 60-degree wedge on the circular watch face. The concept of 10 minutes had a distinctly spatial feel to it. An hour had a certain wholeness or completeness. An hour of digital time, however, is just another number. To see how late you are in digital time, you must add and subtract. If you're not good at arithmetic, digital time can be problematic.

3 Digital time may even be processed in a different portion of the brain than spatial time. Spatial concepts tend to be processed primarily by the right, intuitive hemisphere of the cerebral cortex, but arithmetic concepts are generally handled on the left, or verbal and intellectual, side.

4 "At the very least," says one computer scientist of the advent of digital time, "the terms 'clockwise' and 'counterclockwise' will lose their meaning."

5 In the digital age, changes in our perception of time will be subtle but pervasive. Time, after all, is a human invention to keep people and machines the world over (and eventually the cosmos over) in step with

141

each other. How we conceive of time, how we record it and how our brains process it cannot but affect our view of our place in the Universe.

6   And if the inexpensive digital watch can influence our lives to such an extent, what of the home computer, the pocket computer, the two-way wrist television or some as-yet-unknown technological miracle that will become commonplace in the next few decades?

7   In less than 40 years, the image of the mathematics professor tending an electronic "brain" has been replaced by the teenager navigating a video spaceship through a simulated asteroid field. The computing power that once filled entire buildings and was formerly available only to universities, government and big businesses now fits into everyone's pocket, thanks to the development of the microprocessor—an entire computer on a tiny silicon chip. Digital technology has made possible such advances in computer speed and such miniaturization that, for Madison Avenue, the term "digital" has become the updated version of "new and improved." Advertisements tout not only digital watches but digital musical recordings and even computerized auto ignitions and washing machines.

8   The digital age is said to hold out dazzling promise: the drudgery of the assembly line and of clerical work will be greatly reduced or disappear entirely as computers take over "intelligent tasks"; tremendous savings in energy will occur when computers control heating and cooling; pictures, voices, music and data will travel distortion-free over thousands of miles at low cost.

9   But while computer experts readily recite long lists of technological triumphs just over the horizon, surprisingly few look deeper into the effects of the digital age on the human psyche. When I contacted one huge computer corporation seeking scientists interested in discussing how their creations might change human consciousness, it was suggested that I might better contact "some of the science-fiction boys."

Our culture has no precedent for the strange gifts computer science offers—or threatens—to bestow upon us.

10   But as Seymour Papert, professor of mathematics and education at the Massachusetts Institute of Technology, points out, even some science-fiction writers haven't looked very deeply. "Millions of 'Star Trek' fans know the starship *Enterprise* has a computer that gives rapid and accurate answers to complex questions posed to it," he writes in *Mindstorms: Children, Computers and Powerful Ideas*. "But no attempt is made in 'Star Trek' to suggest that the human characters aboard think in ways very different from the manner in which people in the twentieth century think. Contact with the computer has not, as far as we are allowed to see in these episodes, changed how these people think about themselves or how they approach problems."

11   But a few scientists like Papert have thought about the implications of computer technology on human life, and their view of humanity in the digital age is of a species vastly different from the one we know today. For example, Marvin Minsky, professor in the departments of electrical engineering and computer science at MIT and one of the founders of the field of artificial intelligence, sees the coming digital age as the next step in human evolution. "Our culture has no precedent for the strange gifts that computer science offers—or threatens—to bestow upon us," he adds.

12   Derek de Solla Price, professor of the history of science at Yale University, insists that the past gives only a hint of things to come: "We're only at the very beginning of centuries of change. Whole new classes of technologies are going to develop." Among the developments Price foresees: programmerless computers, new types of human-machine relationships requiring no keyboarding—even the makings of mental telepathy.

13   "We're like cavemen with fire in our relationship with the computer," says Lee Thomas of Bell Laboratories. Thomas is a developer of the Belmac-32A, a microprocessor with the equivalent of 150,000 transistors on a single silicon chip. Thomas is enthusiastic about computer technology: "It's all the more exciting if you've worked in it all your life," he observes. But he's quick to add, "Everything we do nowadays with the computer is obvious. We've always had some sort of calculator, for example, whether an abacus or a mechanical device. So now we've

equipped the calculator with a microprocessor. True innovation will come only when we do something with this fantastic technology we've never done before. Imagination is more limited than technology."

14   Some scientists characterize people today as immigrants in a new land dominated by digital technology. Like all recent arrivals they will depend on their old points of reference and speak with an accent—the accent of what has been termed the precomputer epoch.

15   Thomas feels that future generations will be the first to achieve true computer literacy. "The real impact of things like video games has been to get kids hooked on this digital technology," he says. "We've bred a generation that is not burdened by preconceived notions that the computer is some exotic and expensive piece of equipment to be nurtured by high priests." Thomas sees young people with their home computers as having the same relationship to technology as their counterparts who once constructed crystal radios on the kitchen table. The first large-scale use that adults made of the radio was to broadcast music and news, he points out. "But that was just refining the already existing orchestra and newspaper modes. Those kids with their crystal sets took the technology—the radio wave—and turned it into radar, television and globe-spanning communication satellites."

16   Tom Landauer, who heads a group at Bell Labs studying how people react when they encounter technological change, draws an analogy between the onset of the computer age and the invention of the printing press in the 1400s. "Gutenberg had found a way of capturing, storing and disseminating information," he notes. "It was to have an enormous influence. But it was nearly four hundred years before that innovation was effectively exploited as an everyday medium." The obstacle? Literacy had not become widespread.

17   "I was first exposed to computers in college," says one engineer. "And in a way that was pretty early. But my kids—one, six years old and the other, nine—think nothing of sitting down at our home computer and writing little programs for themselves. As a professional in the field, I think that kind of sophistication is mind-boggling."

AFTER THE FIRST READING ━━━━━━━━━

The author is primarily concerned about: (Check one.)

_____ 1. The differences between spatial time and digital time.

_____ 2. The deeper effects of the digital age on the human psyche.

Read the selection again. Then, go on to the section Building Reading Skills.

BUILDING READING SKILLS ━━━━━━━━━━

Understanding the Organization

You were correct if you selected number 2 in After the First Reading.

1. The article begins by contrasting spatial and digital time. What are some of the features of each? (See paragraphs 1–8). Enter the items in the proper columns.

spatial time   *digital time*

2. *Then, the author asks the important question. In what paragraph does the author state the main point of the article? Highlight the sentence which contains the point.*

   in paragraph _____

   How does he go about investigating the question?

   _____

Interviewing the Experts

Do close reading to find which statement was made by each of the "science-fiction boys" whose names are listed here. Place the correct letter in front of the quotation:

a) Seymour Papert   b) Marvin Minsky   c) Lee Thomas
          d) Derek de Solla Price   e) Tom Landauer

_____ 1. "It was nearly four hundred years before that innovation (the printing press) was effectively exploited as an everyday medium."

_____ 2. "We've bred a generation that is not burdened by preconceived notions that the computer is some exotic and expensive piece of equipment . . ."

_____ 3. "We're like cavemen with fire in our relationship with the computer."

_____ 4. "Our culture has no precedent for the strange gifts that computer science offers—or threatens—to bestow on us."

_____ 5. "We're only at the very beginning of centuries of change. Whole new classes of technologies are going to develop."

_____ 6. "No attempt is made in 'Star Trek' to suggest that the human characters aboard (the Starship Enterprise) think in ways very different
from the manner in which people in the twentieth century think."

_____ 7. "True innovation will come only when we do something with this
fantastic technology we've never done before. Imagination is more
limited than technology."

Reinforcing New Vocabulary

The article contains almost ten phrases and expressions which contain the word
digital. How many can you find? Enter them below:

Expression with *digital*   paragraph

TALKING/WRITING ABOUT ⎯⎯⎯⎯⎯⎯⎯⎯

1. In a group, discuss these ideas:
   - What is your reaction to the quotation below from the article? (para-
     graph 4)

   "Some scientists characterize people today as immigrants in a new land
   dominated by digital technology. Like all recent arrivals, they will depend
   on their old points of reference and speak with an accent—the accent of
   what has been termed the precomputer epoch."
   - What have you done to become 'computer literate'?
   - What is the relationship between the digital age and artificial intelligence
     (A-I)?

2. Write a report on your personal experience with the computer:
   - What effect has it had on your life?
   - What have been the positive and negative aspects?
   - Consider the question from two points of view:
     a) directly   (do you use a computer for word processing?)
     b) indirectly   (what services do you receive that make use of comput-
                      ers? banks, shops, vehicle registration, school rec-
                      ords . . .)

The Big Momma

A Note About . . .

Written by a top-ranking science-writer, this article appeared in an airlines magazine. On airplanes, readers expect to be entertained when they pick up the free magazine they find in their seat pocket. *The Big Momma* contains solid information, but still has a light tone.

BEFORE READING

To Think About:

1. Read the title: How can you tell that the article will have a light tone? Who is "momma?"

2. Read the subtitle: How does it explain the meaning of the title? Who is the one primeval woman? What field of science do geneticists work in?

3. Adjust your reading for your own purpose. Not all readers need to understand the paragraphs containing technical information. Many airplane readers would skip over them, simply reading for the most important idea.

Vocabulary Preparation

1. These key words appear in the article in various forms and in combinations with other words. Check the meaning of each by using your English-English dictionary.

genetics, genes, geneticists
lineage, genealogical line

2. These words and expressions are thematically related to each other. Which ones do you already know?

ancestral, ancestor	family tree
branches of descent	offspring
descended, descendant	predecessor
diverge	prehistory
evolution	primeval
	species

147

3. Technical Vocabulary: You will understand these terms in a general way from your reading of the article. To increase your knowledge, look up each one in an encyclopedia before reading.

DNA	Neanderthal
mitochondria	Homo Erectus
placenta	

To Look For:

1. The writer based his information on interviews with five scientists. As you read, look for their names and the work associated with each one.

2. Do the scientists all agree with each other?

3. What scientific discovery about the divergence of man and apes was made more than twenty years ago?

The Big Momma

Are all humans descended from one primeval woman? Some geneticists think so.

By Robert Ebisch

1 THE BIBLE is right: Eve, the ancestral mother of the human race, was real.

2 She lived, according to recent calculations, 250,000 years ago. She was not the only woman of her time, but something about her was special. Every human being on earth— whether black, Caucasian, Oriental, American Indian, or Australian aborigine—is her direct descendant. At long last the Family of Man, peering deep into the structure of its own genes, has found its mom.

3 Mom's bones may still lie buried somewhere in Africa or the Middle East, where she is believed to have lived. And she may have a modern-day equivalent; some woman among us, even now, may be giving birth to the future of the human race.

4 Such are some of the startling ideas that arise from a new and rapidly developing field of scientific detective work in which the genetic make-up of today's populations is thought to provide clues to those of generations past. That a person's gross features, such as hair and eye color, are genetically determined is old news. Blood typing, discovered in the last century, is another common example of ancestral evidence. In recent decades, however, a vast array of human proteins have been enlisted to aid biologists, archaeologists, and linguists in their search for the threads of lineage.

5 "For a long time, many people argued that Australian aborigines and Melanesians were related to Africans," says anthropologist Vincent Sarich of the University of California at Berkeley, "but blood-group data shows they're not. People used to think that the African Bushmen were Oriental in origin because their facial features *seemed* Oriental, but analysis of blood proteins shows that they're hyper-African—that is, they differ from other races in the same ways that Africans do, only more so."

6 In 1967, Sarich delivered a knock-out punch to the dogma—widely accepted in his field—that humans and apes diverged at least 20 million years ago. Working in the lab of Berkeley geneticist Allan C. Wilson, Sarich examined structural differences in serum albumin, a protein found in both humans and African apes. Random mutations change DNA, the long-chain molecule that forms our genetic blueprint, and in turn those mutations alter the proteins that are built from "instructions" embedded in the DNA. These changes take place at a more or less steady rate over time. Sarich established a rate by looking at the evolution of serum albumin in other species whose divergence from common ancestors is more clearly documented in the fossil record. Then, comparing that rate with the serum albumin differences of humans and apes, he de-

termined that they had diverted "only" 5 million years ago. Fellow anthropologists didn't warm to the idea overnight, he says, but a date of 4 to 10 million years ago for the divorce between apes and humans is now widely accepted.

7   Scientists are no longer restricted to analysis of hereditary protein differences caused by DNA mutations; today, direct analysis of DNA is possible. Biologists can now read the DNA molecule like a book, and though on some of its "pages" the print is still blurred or reads like a foreign language, its story is becoming increasingly legible.

8   Researchers are using computers to systematize the incredibly complex genetic code. Ten years hence, any large medical center may well be able to display on computer screens the DNA sequences of 5,000 people to aid in the diagnosis and treatment of their biological malfunctions. Some 2,000 inherited diseases can already be diagnosed prenatally through inspections of a fetus's DNA.

9   The DNA that resides in the nucleus of each cell and determines our heredity, however, gets scrambled in every new generation, when the DNA of mother and father mix to produce an offspring. Nuclear DNA can reveal much about the relation of one species to another, but this scrambling obscures the trail of lineages within populations of that species.

10   What made it possible to locate Mom was another kind of DNA contained in blobby little organisms called *mitochondria*. Mitochondria inhabit, by the thousands, every human, animal, and insect cell. The mitochondrion is believed to have invaded the cells of our progenitors as a parasite about a billion years ago, when those progenitors were themselves single-cell organisms. Today mitochondria are the powerhouses of our cells, using the oxygen we breathe to burn the nutrients we eat, and thus producing most of our energy. At the same time, they are dependent on us, having given up the ability to survive without our cellular machinery. But they did not give up their own, separate store of DNA. They reproduce on their own schedule inside our cells, independent of human reproduction.

11   In 1980, Douglas Wallace, a geneticist with the department of biochemistry at Emory University in Atlanta, discovered that the mitochondrion is a genetic heirloom passed intact from one generation to another through women. The mitochondria in our bodies all descend from those mitochondria in the single egg cell from which we were formed. Mitochondrial DNA—mDNA—is not scrambled from one generation to another, but retains a genetic message that has passed down, clear and unaltered, from the otherwise murky confusion of prehistory. A man's mDNA never even reaches his own children. A woman's mDNA, however, is immortal.

12   "This was very important," Wallace says, "the foundation for all subsequent work on mitochondrial DNA: a DNA specific for the female lineage. The only way mitochondrial DNA can change is by progressive accumulation of mutations." This accumulation, researchers have discovered, is as regular as clockwork, taking place at the

same rate for fish and fowl, beast and bug: random accidents of nature change about two percent of the mDNA molecule every million years. It was that regularity that sent Berkeley geneticist Rebecca Cann off in search of Mom in 1981.

13 Cann obtained the placentas of 112 women, from a variety of races, who had given birth in San Francisco hospitals. Placentas are a rich source of mitochondria. Studying the differences in the women's mDNA—and using the belief that these differences accumulate at a rate of two percent per million years—computer analysis traced them all, black, white, and Oriental, back to a single ancestor who lived 300,000 to 150,000 years ago. "We usually say 250,000 years," says Cann, who is now with the department of genetics at the University of Hawaii.

14 MOM MAY have been a Neanderthal.

She may even have been a Homo erectus, Neanderthal's predecessor, for the transition between those early hominid forms is usually placed about 300,000 years ago. But, despite the fact that Mom's appearance would not have qualified her for the cheerleading squad, she was not the ugly, stupid, hairy brute of popular fancy. Our sainted mother was a woman of culture.

15 Homo erectus was the first hominid to spread out of Africa to Europe and Asia, and the first to discover fire and put it to constructive use. Homo erectus made great advances in the creation of artificial environments through sheltered spaces, clothing himself (or *her*self) in animal skins, and cooking meat and possibly grain. Homo erectus sites in Spain show signs of organized hunting and butchering of big game in the vicinity of oval huts, stone hearths, and tools of stone and wood.

16 Why do all our genes trace back to a mother who lived 250,000 years ago, near the transition between Homo erectus and Neanderthal? Could Mom, in fact, have been the Homo erectus who gave birth to a Neanderthal, a beetle-browed genius the like of which had never walked the earth?

17 Culturally, perhaps mentally, Homo erectus was a dim bulb compared with Neanderthal. Yet Vincent Sarich thinks the difference between Homo erectus and Neanderthal was mainly cultural. "Homo erectus isn't a thing," he says. "It's a phase. It grades into what we call Neanderthal, and where you make that break [between them] is arbitrary. Neanderthals should really be seen as terminal Homo erectus."

18 Even in the evolution from one species to another, the transition occurs not through one individual but through many, over a period of time. Mom was undoubtedly part of some small population group from which her mitochondrial line spread, eventually to supplant all others on the face of the earth. But what could have happened 300,000 years ago to bring this change about?

19 "This is where Allan [Wilson] and Becky [Cann] and I don't agree on the interpretation of the data," Sarich says. "The problem is that there isn't any break in the fossil record or archaeological record at the period of

time where they have this 'Eve.' As far as I can tell, nothing happened 300,000 years ago."

20   Although a rate of two percent change in mDNA every million years has been shown for a variety of life forms, Sarich is one of several researchers who think that the rate may be different for humans. Humans, whose large brains drive their evolution at a more rapid rate than that of other creatures, may be a special case. If the rate of mDNA change in humans were half as fast as in chimpanzees, Sarich says, Cann's calculations might bump Mom back a few hundred thousand more years to the time when Homo erectus, limited to sub-Saharan Africa, began spreading to Europe and Asia.

"There," Sarich says, "you would have an event to which you could tie the radiation of that mitochondria to the rest of the Old World."

22   Cann, for her part, says, "I'm a little more optimistic than Vince on our mitochondrial DNA data. This particular gene pool could have arisen in Africa and stayed there for some time. It may not have spread until 100,000 years ago, when there is some archaeological evidence for cultural advance."

23   The spread of Mom's mitochondrial DNA is not necessarily tied to a transition from one species to another, or even to the spread of humans out of Africa. According to Douglas Wallace of Emory University, it could have been a mere matter of chance that her genetic line continued and others died out. If a mother has two children, they may comprise two boys, a girl and a boy, or two girls. That means there's a 50 percent chance that the mitochondrial line will end in any one offspring. "From the mitochondrial DNA point of view," Wallace says, "a family with two boys is dead. You can lose lineages rapidly."

24   It is possible, of course, that the mDNA of one woman who lives today, through millenniums of statistical attrition, could become the mDNA of some future edition of humanity. In the small populations of humans long past, such attrition could easily have brought one lineage to the fore. Mom's line may just have had a little more pluck and a lot more luck than those of her contemporaries, and may not have been in the vanguard of the exodus from Africa.

25   Wallace, in fact, believes that Mom is more likely to have lived in Europe or Asia than in Africa. The organization of Mom's original mDNA, he says, is found in only 13 percent of Africans, but in more than 80 percent of Asians and Europeans. "Our data suggests that mDNA today is more likely traced to an origin in Asia," he says, "and from there it radiated back to Europe and Africa."

26   This idea, in turn, conflicts with the views of Cann and some of her colleagues. Mark Stoneking, a graduate student in Allan Wilson's lab at Berkeley, is now using mDNA to investigate the origins of aboriginal New Guineans, but he's also worked with Cann on the search for Mom. There is evidence, Stoneking says, that Mom's family tree has two primary branches of descent: the first leading to some modern Africans, the second leading

to all Asians, all Caucasians, and some other modern Africans. Other evidence, he says, suggests that African mDNA shows more diversity than that of other races. The longer a race has been around, in other words, the more changes its mDNA will show; thus African mDNA is older.

27 "If you had Africans moving to Europe in the distant past and all Europeans descended from that," Stoneking explains, "that's how you'd get a younger date for Caucasians as a whole."

28 Future research may refine our ideas about the time and place Mom lived. But the mere idea that she existed throws a warm, new light on human history. Despite all of our differences of race, religion, and culture, and all the hostilities those differences cause; despite all our weapons and wars and brutalities, we are still brothers and sisters descended together from The Great Mom.

29 Now if only she'd come back and box a few ears. □

Robert Ebisch is our regular Science columnist. He lives in Boulder, Colorado.

AFTER THE FIRST READING ━━━━

What is the important new theory about earliest man which is reported in the article? What role does DNA play in the theory? Be ready to explain the main idea in the article to your partner or in a small group.

Read the selection again. Then, go on to the section Building Reading Skills.

BUILDING READING SKILLS ━━━━

Quoting from Sources

The writer synthesized the work of five geneticists. Match each with his/her contributions as cited in the article. Use scanning strategies to find the paragraphs in which the work is mentioned.

a) Vincent Sarich   b) Allan C. Wilson   c) Douglas Wallace

d) Rebecca Cann   e) Mark Stoneking

1. _____ Over 20 years ago, established the rate of change in serum albumin, a protein found in humans and apes, by looking at other species whose divergence is established in the fossil record. (para. _____)

2. _____ Dated the divergence of men and apes to four–ten million years ago. (para. _____)

3. _____ Discovered that mDNA is a genetic heirloom passed from one generation to another through the female lineage. (para. _____)

4. _____ Discovered that a woman's mDNA is immortal; it doesn't die out. (para. _____)

5. _____ Hypothesized that in mDNA change over time is as regular as clock work. (para. _____)

6. _____ Studied human, female placentas. Using computer analysis, traced them back to a single ancestor. (para. _____)

7. _____ Believes the first "momma" was not clearly either Homo Erectus or Neanderthal. (para. _____)

8. _____ Because of the absence of fossil record evidence, does not agree with the hypothesis that the first woman lived 300,000 years ago. (para. _____)

9. _____ Thinks that humans' mDNA change rate is different from other life forms. (para. _____)

10. _____ Believes the first woman lived in Europe or Asia, not Africa. (para. _____)

11. _____ Through mDNA analysis, wants to establish that man had two branches of descent. (para. _____)

Checking on Understanding

If you are reading to understand details, quiz yourself by checking all the statements which are true:

_____ Men and apes diverged about four–ten million years ago.

_____ Mitochondria DNA and computer analyses helped scientists hypothesize that the first human female lived about 250,000 years ago.

_____ The rate of change in mDNA is the same for all species.

_____ All the scientists quoted in the article agree about the time and place where "the big momma" lived.

The Writer's Research

The author of the article did more than just synthesize scientists' work. Since one of the important questions which geneticists continue to investigate involves both the location and approximate date of the earliest woman, he wanted to give readers a sense of the time and place of Homo Erectus and Neanderthal. To do so, he probably consulted an encyclopedia too.

Find the paragraphs that present information about Homo Erectus and Neanderthal. How is it the same, or different from what you read in an encyclopedia? Write a summary of the information in the article about Homo Erectus and Neanderthal. Use your own sources of information as well.

Reinforcing Vocabulary

1. The word *genetic* and all its variations is a key term in the article. Often it appears before another noun, modifying it.

    For example, *genetic code* para. _____
    Find other examples. Write them here:

    _____

2. *Lineage* is also a key term. It occurs as a head noun, with modifiers preceeding it.

    For example: *trail of lineages* para. _____
    Find other examples. Write them here:

    _____

3. What other words or expressions can you find which are related to *genetic*, both in form and meaning? Write them here:

    For example: *generations past* para. _____

TALKING/WRITING ABOUT ━━━━━━━━━━

1. The article presents a view of how scientists share ideas, contribute to each other's work, and make critical comments about each other's work.

    In your group, discuss what you know about the ways in which scientific work is carried out. What did you learn from the article about the ways in which scientists give comments about their colleagues' ideas? What surprised you? Do you think that these five geneticists know each other personally?

2. Popular comics and other non-scientific writings often present curious information about prehistoric people. For example, they show early man living side-by-side with dinosaurs.

    Find examples from either TV programs or comic pages in the newspapers. Write a criticism of these depictions using information about Neanderthal and Homo Erectus which you found in an encyclopedia and in the article.

    _____

Making A Chimp Out of Man

A Note About . . .

Jared Diamond is a professor of physiology at UCLA who writes popular science for *Discover* magazine in which this article appeared. Unlike what you would find in a scientific paper in a professional journal, in this article the author brings together ideas from many fields and then presents his own ethically-based concerns.

BEFORE READING _____

To Think About:

1. Read the title. It contains a double meaning by sounding like the popular expression, "to make a monkey out of someone," or to make someone appear foolish. *Chimp* is a short form of *chimpanzee*. You can guess that the article will deal with _____ and _____.

2. Read the subtitle: *to be taken aback* is to be strongly surprised or shocked. What else can you guess about the contents of the article?

chim•pan•zee, *n.* an anthropoid ape of Africa, with black hair and large outstanding ears; it is smaller and less fierce than a gorilla, and is noted for its intelligence (*Webster's New Twentieth Century Dictionary Unabridged*, 1978 Collins World)

Vocabulary Preparation

All of the scientific fields listed below are mentioned in the article. Use your English-English dictionary to become familiar with the meaning of each. Then, match the field with the correct descriptive phrase associated with it. Many of the descriptive phrases also occur in the article.

a) anthropology   b) biology   c) comparative anatomy
d) evolutionary biology   e) genetics   f) linguistics
g) molecular biology   h) ornithology   i) paleontology
j) taxonomy

_____ 1. fossil or geological evidence

_____ 2. hierarchical categories, subspecies . . . phylum, each further apart than the next

_____ 3. Darwinian-derived theories of changes in species

_____ 4. the evolutionary relationship among birds

_____ 5. DNA, a long chain of smaller molecules whose sequence carries genetic information

_____ 6. the science of heredity and genes; studies genetic mutations

_____ 7. generalizations about mankind

_____ 8. man belongs in a separate family because of certain traits such as large brain, bipedal posture

_____ 9. language as systems

_____ 10. characteristics such as brain size, upright posture, amount of body hair

To Look For:

During the first reading, try to find the main ideas. Looking for answers to these questions will aid you.

1. The author says that as a species, man is *egocentric* (regarding oneself as the center of everything). What does this mean? How does the article illustrate this idea?

2. What is a DNA clock?

3. How has it been used to understand the family relationship between man and other apes, living and extinct?

Making A Chimp Out of Man

*Even Darwin himself might have been taken aback if he had known
how closely we are related to the apes*

By Jared Diamond

1 WE ARE egocentric as a species, not just as individuals. Yes, we find it interesting to read about the evolutionary relationships of fossil horses, but what we really care about is *our* evolutionary relationships. Hence we have every reason to be excited by the dramatic new insights into our ancestry produced only within the past year by a technique of molecular biology called the DNA clock. Scientists are finding out that we are even more closely related to apes than anyone imagined. This bit of news will surely alter our view of ourselves and apes, just as Darwin's *Origin of Species* did.

2 Biologists, of course, have long realized that we, like apes, are primates, and that chimpanzees and gorillas are our closest kin. (The other living apes are orangutans and gibbons.) Virtually every biologist puts man and apes together in one super-family, the Hominoidea. Nevertheless, the details of our relationships have remained the subject of an intense scientific debate, which boils down to three questions:

1. What is the family tree of relationships among man, living apes, and extinct ancestral apes?

2. Just how similar are we, genetically, to apes?

3. When did we and the closest ape last share a common ancestor?

3 Comparative anatomy once thought it had answered the first two questions. Although human beings look like chimpanzees and gorillas, they differ from them in obvious features like brain size, upright posture, and amount of body hair, as well as in many subtler points. However, on closer evaluation these anatomical facts failed to solve even the first question. Depending on what anatomical characteristics they consider important and how they interpret them, different biologists within the past decade have had different favorites among five alternative ancestral trees (see the illustration on page 159).

4 While biologists agree that gibbons are the most distinct living apes and were the first to diverge from the hominoid tree, they differ as to whether the next branch to break away was the orangutan (the majority view) or man (a minority view). Most biologists have thought that gorillas and chimpanzees are more like each other than either is like us, implying that we branched off before the gorilla and chimpanzee diverged from each other (tree number 2 in the illustration). Others have considered humans closest to gorillas (tree 3), or closest to chimpanzees (tree 1), or humans and gorillas and chimpanzees equidistant from each other (tree 4). In any case, anatomy addresses nei-

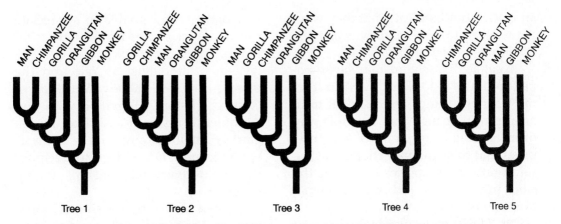

Possible family trees showing the evolution of primates: Although anatomists have traditionally favored tree 2, other studies have suggested at least four other trees with different branching patterns. The molecular clock used by Sibley and Ahlquist indicates that tree 1 is the correct one. In this evolutionary time-table, man appears to have tumbled from the exalted status he assigned himself.

ther the third question, about when we diverged from apes, nor the second, about genetic distance. What anatomist can say whether we differ from gorillas in 0.1 per cent, 0.5 per cent, or 50 per cent of our genes?

5   In principle, the questions of dating and of the correct ancestral tree could be solved by fossil evidence. But hominoid fossils are few and fragmentary, and often difficult to date accurately. Estimates by paleontologists have man branching from the apes between four million and 19 million years ago. On the question of genetic distance, fossil evidence is as silent as are anatomical studies of living apes.

6   About 25 years ago, biologists began thinking about a "molecular clock" by which to measure genetic distances and date evolutionary branching points. The idea was as follows: Sup-

pose there were a molecule that occurred in many or all species, and whose structure slowly changed (because of genetic mutations) at the same steady rate. Two species derived from a common ancestor would start off with identical forms of the molecule, but as they diverged from each other and from the ancestor, mutations would change it. Thus by comparing the present architecture of the molecule in different species, we could measure how different the creatures were genetically and how much time had elapsed since their divergence.

7   For instance, a molecule might differ by one per cent in a pair of species known from fossil evidence to have diverged five million years ago. If the same molecule differed by two per cent between two species whose fossil histories were unknown, the molecu-

lar clock would indicate that they went their separate evolutionary ways ten million years ago.

8   Neat as this scheme may be on paper, putting it to work was another matter. Four things are essential to it: an appropriate molecule; a simple way of measuring changes in its structure; proof that this structure changes at the same rate in all species (*i.e.*, that the clock runs steady); and an idea of what that rate is.

9   BY 1970 molecular biologists had settled on two of the key elements. They found that the best molecule is DNA (deoxyribonucleic acid), a long chain made up of smaller molecules whose sequence carries all the genetic information transmitted from parents to offspring. (There are clocks based on proteins, but these have several disadvantages.) They also determined that a quick measure of changes in DNA's structure could be made by mixing DNA from two species, and determining how many degrees the melting point of the brew was reduced below the melting point of DNA from a single species. As it turns out, a melting point lowered by one degree Celsius (abbreviated: delta T = one degree) means that the DNA of the two species differs by about one per cent.

10   But the DNA clock's two other elements—proof of a steady rate of change and measurement of that rate—were more elusive. They required taxonomists willing to undertake the drudgery of obtaining DNA and measuring delta T values for many species, and most taxonomists were unfamiliar with the nuances of molec-ular biology and unable to appreciate the potential power of the new technique. An exception was Charles Sibley, an ornithologist at Yale and the director of its Peabody Museum of Natural History. Together with Jon Ahlquist, a research associate, he began an ambitious program of analysis with the new DNA clock to decipher the evolutionary relationships among birds.

11   In ten years they examined more than a thousand bird species, and showed that the rate of DNA evolution—the rate at which the genetic molecules change—is the same for all species. Thus, the clock runs steady. To calibrate the clock, Sibley and Ahlquist used pairs of avian species for which they knew both the delta T values and how long ago the birds split apart on the evolutionary tree, according to independent fossil or geological evidence. These calibrations suggested that a delta T value of one degree Celsius in the DNA corresponds to a divergence time of about four and a half million years.

12   The methodical effort by Sibley and Ahlquist was a monumental achievement, but it remains in dispute. One part of the problem is that their methods are still unfamiliar; another part is that their conclusions about bird relationships disagree in some cases with those reached by traditional anatomical methods. Here are typical reactions from some of my scientist friends:

"I'm sick of hearing about that stuff. I no longer pay attention to anything those guys write." (An anatomist)

"Their methods are okay, but why would anyone want to do something so boring as all that bird taxonomy?" (A molecular biologist)

"Their conclusions need a lot of testing by other methods before we can believe them." (An evolutionary biologist)

"Their results are the Revealed Truth, and you better believe it." (A geneticist)

13 My own assessment is that the last view will turn out to be the most nearly correct. The principles on which the DNA clock rests are unassailable; Sibley and Ahlquist's methods are state of the art; and the internal consistency of their measurements on more than 18,000 pairs of bird species supports their results.

14 SIBLEY and Ahlquist have not proceeded hastily. Just as Darwin had the good sense to marshal his evidence for the evolution of Galapagos finches before going on to discuss the descent of man, so they have stuck prudently to birds for most of their work with the DNA clock. Only in recent years have they begun to apply the same DNA methods to human origins, comparing our genetic molecules with those of our closest relatives: the chimpanzee (*Pan troglodytes*), the pygmy chimpanzee (*Pan paniscus*), the gorilla (*Gorilla gorilla*), the orangutan (*Pongo pygmaeus*), two species of gibbon (the common gibbon *Hylobates lar* and the siamang gibbon *Hylobates syndactylus*), and five species of Old World monkeys.

15 Not surprisingly, they found the biggest mismatches between monkey DNA and the DNA of man or of the apes. This result was in agreement with the prevailing view, based mainly on anatomical evidence, that monkeys belong to a separate primate family. Similarly, Sibley and Ahlquist confirmed the accepted wisdom that the chimpanzee and pygmy chimpanzee are very closely related: their DNAs have a delta T of only 0.7 degrees Celsius, the lowest mismatch of any of the primates.

16 The genetic distance between man and either chimpanzee species (1.9 degrees) is more than double that between the two chimpanzees. However, the gorilla is still further from man or from either of the two chimps (2.1 to 2.4 degrees Celsius). Consequently, the gorilla must have branched from our common family tree slightly before we separated from the chimpanzees. This means that the correct tree is the first, not the second, which is the one usually favored by scientists. Put another way, the chimpanzee's closest relative is not the gorilla but man!

17 What do these results imply about our position in the animal kingdom? Biologists classify living things in hierarchical categories, each further apart than the next, in this sequence: subspecies, species, genus, family, superfamily, order, class, and phylum. The *Encyclopaedia Britannica* and all the biology texts on my shelf say that man and the apes belong to the same order, Primates, and the same superfamily, Hominoidea, but to separate families. Hominidae and Pongidae. Whether Sibley's and Ahlquist's work changes this classification depends on one's philosophy of taxonomy.

18   Traditional taxonomists group species into broader categories (genus, family, and so on) by making somewhat subjective evaluations of how important the differences between species are. Such taxonomists place man in a separate family because of distinctive functional traits like large brain and bipedal posture, and this classification would remain unaffected by measures of genetic distance.

19   Another school of taxonomy, called cladistics (from *klados*, the Greek word for branch), argues that classification should be objective and uniform, based on genetic distance or times of divergence. All taxonomists agree, for instance, that common and siamang gibbons belong together in the genus *Hylobates*. Yet these species are genetically more distant, and diverged longer ago, than did man, chimpanzees, and the gorilla. On this basis man should be put in the same genus as chimpanzees and the gorilla. Furthermore, since the genus name *Homo* is the oldest, by the rules of zoological nomenclature it takes priority over the new names *Pan* and *Gorilla*. Conclusion: Not one but four species of genus *Homo* exist on earth today—the gorilla, *Homo gorilla*; the two chimpanzees, *Homo troglodytes* and *Homo paniscus*; and man, *Homo sapiens*.

20   For years, traditional taxonomy reinforced our anthropocentric tendencies by claiming to see a fundamental dichotomy between mighty man, standing alone on high, and the lowly apes all together in the abyss of bestiality. Now our pre-eminence is challenged. The new results do not specify how we *should* think about man and apes, or tell us about our respective places in the universe. But they will probably influence how we do think. I can envision several areas that might be affected.

21   One area concerns how we use apes. At present we draw a distinction between animals and man, and this distinction guides our ethical code and actions. For example, it is acceptable to exhibit caged apes in zoos and to subject them to lethal experiments for purposes of medical research, but it is not acceptable to do the same with humans. I wonder how the public will feel when the label on the zoo cage reads *"Homo gorilla"* or *"Homo troglodytes."*

22   Even now our treatment of apes poses difficult ethical problems, not a simple choice between good and evil. Without the sympathetic interest in apes that many people gain at zoos, there might be less financial support for efforts to protect apes in the wild. Experiments with chimpanzees are playing an irreplaceable role in developing a vaccine against AIDS and in testing a vaccine against malaria. Having watched and thought about chimpanzees, I don't like sacrificing them for research. Having been sick with malaria and having lived among people decimated by malaria, I also don't like malaria. Are we Americans entitled to tell African nations, where close to a million people die of malaria each year, that those people are less important than chimpanzees?

23   ANOTHER area affected by our attitudes concerns what we notice in apes. Contrary to the popular stereotype, scientists do not

faithfully record whatever happens to be going on before their eyes. What usually interests them depends on where their expectations tell them to go, and what they look for there, and whether they consider what they see worth paying attention to. For too long we neglected looking into ape societies for traits considered quintessentially human, like language and culture. The recent exciting discoveries of tool use, capacity for learning artificial languages, incest taboos, and invention of new behavior in chimpanzees or gorillas were made possible by changed attitudes and expectations as well as by patient observing. What else do apes do that we have not thought to look for?

24   I predict that we will seek and discover great behavioral differences, transmitted from each generation to the next, among troops of wild chimpanzees or gorillas: in short, cultural differences. All anthropologists know that generalizations about mankind based on study of Californians may break down for New Yorkers or Tanzanians. Yet we persist in talking about "behavior of wild chimpanzees," forgetting that most of our notions are based on one troop studied by Jane Goodall along the shores of Lake Tanganyika.

25   Another prediction; wild chimpanzees and gorillas will prove to have "natural languages"—many vocalizations with meanings that differ among troops. While captive chimpanzees and gorillas have been taught systems of symbolic communication based on tokens or hand signs, anthropocentric linguists object to describing these systems as languages. They insist that it would be a wasted effort to look for a rich, sound-based system of communication in apes; the anatomy of the ape throat supposedly makes this impossible. Yet consider what Dorothy Cheney and Robert Seyfarth at UCLA discovered from a sophisticated spectrographic analysis of the grunts uttered by wild monkey troops. What sounded to our untrained ears like an unvarying grunt proved to be a set of different vocalizations, each with a different meaning ("leopard," "snake," "eagle," etc.). An analysis of the grunts of wild gorilla or chimpanzee troops might decipher an even richer language, possibly including names for individual apes.

26   Finally, changes in our attitudes about apes may be crucial in determining whether apes will survive. They are threatened by the destruction of their habitats, and by legal and illegal capture and killing. Within less than a human generation, if trends continue, the mountain gorilla, orangutan, pileated gibbon, Kloss's gibbon, and possibly some other apes as well will exist only in zoos. It is not enough to tell the governments of Uganda, Zaïre, and Indonesia of their moral obligation to protect their wild apes. These are poor countries, and national parks are expensive. If *Homo sapiens* decides that the other members of genus *Homo* are worth saving, *Homo sapiens* in the richer countries will have to bear most of the expense. Perhaps the most important effect of Sibley and Ahlquist's work will be on how we feel about footing that bill to save our closest relatives.

AFTER THE FIRST READING _____

Check all that are correct.

1. We are egocentric as a species, as evidenced by:

    _____ our interest in ourselves

    _____ our view that man is distant from other primates

2. The DNA clock is:

    _____ a technique of molecular biology

    _____ a way of showing the differences between species

    _____ a way of showing the rate of change between species over time

3. By using the DNA clock, some scientists now believe that:

    _____ humans and chimpanzees are more closely related than previously been thought

    _____ the chimp's closest relative is man

Read the selection again. Then, go on to the section Building Reading Skills. Use the questions as a guide for close reading.

BUILDING READING SKILLS _____

Close Reading

Use reading-to-learn strategies by answering questions about each paragraph.

1. Paragraph 1

   The author compares the technique called the DNA clock developed by molecular biologists with Darwin's *Origin of the Species*. Why?

   _____

   _____

2. Paragraph 2
   a) What does the family of Hominoidea include?

   _____

   b) The three main questions which are the center of the scientific debate all focus on the relationship between

   _____ and _____.

3. Paragraphs 3–5

     a) Comparative anatomy is the study of the anatomical structure of animal bodies and their comparison. What did comparative anatomists see as the important differences between human beings and chimpanzees?

       _____

       _____

     b) Why don't biologists agree on the relationship between apes and humans? How many competing family-trees are there? _____

     c) Read paragraph 4. Then look at the illustration of the different trees on page 159. What do biologists agree on? Where do they differ?

       _____

       _____

     d) Why can't paleontology help answer these questions?

       _____

       _____

4. Paragraphs 6–8

     a) What can the "molecular clock" measure? _____

       _____

     b) How can fossil evidence and the "molecular clock" work together? ___

       _____

     c) What is still missing with respect to the rate of change? _____

       _____

5. Paragraphs 9–11

     a) Why is DNA the best molecule to develop a "clock" for? _____

       _____

     b) In using DNA, why were proof of a steady rate of change and measurement of that rate "elusive?" (difficult to find)? _____

       _____

     c) What did Sibley and Ahlquist study in great detail? What important finding did they come up with?

       _____

       _____

6. Paragraphs 12–14

   a) What were two reasons why the work of Sibley and Ahlquist were not fully accepted by other scientists?

   _____   _____

   b) What does the author think of the work of Sibley and Ahlquist? How can they be compared to Darwin?

   _____

   _____

7. Paragraphs 15–19

   a) In applying DNA methods to human origins, Sibley and Ahlquist found the biggest mismatches between

      _____ DNA and the DNA of _____.

   b) Their results also showed that Tree No. _____ is correct. However, most scientists have tended to favor Tree No. _____.

8. Paragraph 20

   a) How has the traditional anthropocentric (anthro = man) view presented the relation between man and apes?

   _____

   _____

   b) Does the author believe that the new view also tells us how we "should"

   look on our species in relation to our "close relatives?" _____

   _____

9. Paragraphs 21–26

   The author outlines four areas which might be effected by the general acceptance of Tree No. 1. Skim these paragraphs and find the major points. List them below:

   a) _____   b) _____

   c) _____   d) _____

10. In what ways do Diamond's (the author's) predictions about future man/ape relations attempt to be free of anthropocentric attitudes?

    _____

    _____

    Do you believe he is successful? _____

TALKING/WRITING ABOUT ────────────

In your group, share your background knowledge and ideas:

1. From reading this article, will you look differently at the animals in the "monkey house" at the zoo the next time you visit there?

2. In what other ways is man anthropocentric?

3. Are you aware of efforts to help save other endangered birds or animals? For example:
   - the whale
   - the dolphin
   - the condor
   - the bald eagle
   - others?

4. Gather information for a written report: Look for books and popular science magazine articles written by or about Jane Goodall who observed a troop of chimpanzees in Tanzania, East Africa. Take notes to use in your written summary.
   - What motivated her to carry out this kind of research?
   - What were some of her principle theories about chimpanzees?

Darwinism Defined: The Difference Between Fact and Theory

A Note About . . .

Stephen Jay Gould is an eminent professor of geology who teaches biology and the history of science at Harvard University. He has published many articles in magazines for non-scientists, along with non-fiction books, including *The Mismeasure of Man* and *Urchin in The Storm*. This segment from a longer piece of writing was intended to clarify the scientific view of Darwinism vs. creationism.

BEFORE READING

To Think About:

1. Read the title: *-ism* is a suffix on nouns meaning a set of principles, beliefs or doctrines. You have already read about Charles Darwin in Unit Two, so guess what the title means.

2. Read paragraph 1: The important verbs are *to establish* and *to propose*.

   • Which is used with facts? _____

   • Which is used with theories? _____

   • *Confidence* is associated with _____

   • *Caution* is associated with _____

Vocabulary Preparation

All of the words below are in the article. Look for them. Which will you add to your Personal Vocabulary-Building Notebook?

incisive	Darwin was a penetrating, incisive thinker; he was a deep thinker.
to infer **inferences**	The method of deriving a judgement in science is usually indirect. *Inferences* are made from the results of past processes without observing actual change.
lexicon	Your Personal Vocabulary-Building Notebook is a dictionary of words and expressions you want to remember and use. In fact, it's a lexicon.
orthodox, **orthodoxy**	Darwin's theory of natural selection became the orthodox, accepted theory among evolutionists in England, but not among scientists in all other countries.

phenomena   observable facts, occurrences (sg.*phenomenon*)

pluralistic   Science thrives on many theories; it is a pluralistic enterprise.

stereotype   The scientific method according to Gould, cannot be reduced to a conventional set of stereotypes, or a list of simple rules.

To Look For:

1. Gould makes a distinction between two aspects of Darwin's work. What are the two claims about evolution which Darwin set out?

2. How does Gould link the two with facts, theories?

3. Gould uses the example of Darwin's work to make a broader statement about the work of scientists. What is Gould's view of science?

Darwinism Defined: The Difference Between Fact and Theory

By Stephen Jay Gould

1 CHARLES DARWIN, who was, perhaps, the most incisive thinker among the great minds of history, clearly divided his life's work into two claims of different character: establishing the fact of evolution, and proposing a theory (natural selection) for the mechanism of evolutionary change. He also expressed, and with equal clarity, his judgment about their different status: confidence in the facts of transmutation and genealogical connection among all organisms, and appropriate caution about his unproved theory of natural selection. He stated in the *Descent of Man*: "I had two distinct objects in view; firstly, to show that species had not been separately created, and secondly, that natural selection had been the chief agent of change . . . If I have erred in . . . having exaggerated its [natural selection's] power . . . I have at least, as I hope, done good service in aiding to overthrow the dogma of separate creations."

2 Darwin wrote those words more than a century ago. Evolutionary biologists have honored his fundamental distinction between fact and theory ever since. Facts are the world's data; theories are explanations proposed to interpret and coordinate facts. The fact of evolution is as well established as anything in science (as secure as the revolution of the earth about the sun), though absolute certainty has no place in our lexicon. Theories, or statements about the causes of documented evolutionary change, are now in a period of intense debate—a good mark of science in its healthiest state. Facts don't disappear while scientists debate theories. As I wrote in an early issue of this magazine "Einstein's theory of gravitation replaced Newton's, but apples did not suspend themselves in mid-air pending the outcome."

3 Since facts and theories are so different, it isn't surprising that these two components of science have had separate histories ever since Darwin. Between 1859 (the year of publication for the *Origin of Species*) and 1882 (the year of Darwin's death), nearly all thinking people came to accept the fact of evolution. Darwin lies beside Newton in Westminster Abbey for this great contribution. His theory of natural selection has experienced a much different, and checkered, history. It attracted some notable followers during his lifetime (Wallace in England, Weismann in Germany), but never enjoyed majority support. It became an orthodoxy among English-speaking evolutionists (but never, to this day, in France or Germany) during the 1930s, and received little cogent criticism until the 1970s. The past fifteen years have wit-

nessed a revival of intense and, this time, highly fruitful debate as scientists discover and consider the implications of phenomena that expand the potential causes of evolution well beyond the unitary focus of strict Darwinism (the struggle for reproductive success among organisms within populations). Darwinian selection will not be overthrown; it will remain a central focus of more inclusive evolutionary theories. But new findings and interpretations at all levels, from molecular change in genes to patterns of overall diversity in geological time, have greatly expanded the scope of important causes—from random, selectively neutral change at the genetic level, to punctuated equilibria and catastrophic mass extinction in geological time. This is a period of vigorous pluralism and intense debate among evolutionary biologists.

4   We learn in high school about *the* scientific method—a cut-and-dried procedure of simplification to essential components, experiment in the controlled situation of a laboratory, prediction and replication. But the sciences of history—not just evolution but a suite of fundamental disciplines ranging from geology, to cosmology, to linguistics—can't operate by this stereotype. We are charged with explaining events of extraordinary complexity that occur but once in all their details. We try to understand the past, but don't pretend to predict the future. We can't see past processes directly, but learn to infer their operation from preserved results.

5   Science is a pluralistic enterprise with a rich panoply of methods appropriate for different kinds of problems. Past events of long duration don't lie outside the realm of science because we cannot make them happen in a month within our laboratory. Direct vision isn't the only, or even the usual, method of inference in science. We don't see electrons, or quarks, or chemical bonds, any more than we see small dinosaurs evolve into birds, or India crash into Asia to raise the Himalayas.

AFTER THE FIRST READING ⸻

1. The two scientific claims in Darwin's body of work were:

    a) ⸻⸻⸻   b) ⸻⸻⸻

2. Which was founded in facts? ⸻⸻⸻⸻⸻⸻

    Which was a theory? ⸻⸻⸻⸻⸻⸻⸻

3. Does Gould believe that descriptions of the scientific method have been simplified? Be ready to explain your answer.

    Read the selection again. Then, go on to the section Building Reading Skills.

BUILDING READING SKILLS ━━━━━━━━━

Understanding Main Ideas

1. In After the First Reading you were correct if you wrote:

    - Darwin established the fact of evolution; he proposed a theory of natural selection.

    In paragraphs 1 and 2: Below are listed words and phrases from the article which make the distinction between fact/theory:

    proposed explanation   world's data   with confidence
        appropriate caution   secure   (under) debate

    Enter each one under the appropriate heading, either *fact* or *theory*, shown below:

    fact   *theory*

2. *In paragraph 3: What has happened to natural selection theory since Darwin's day? Write a brief summary, using the information in paragraph 3.*

3. *In paragraphs 4, 5: The scientific method, according to Gould is or is not a cut-and-dried procedure? Explain your answer by writing a brief paragraph.*

Facts and Theories

From your reading of this and other selections in this Unit, which are a) facts, or b) theories according to the information given in the articles? Place a) or b) in front of each:

1. _____ DNA

2. _____ mitochondrial DNA

3. _____ the first homo erectus was a woman

4. _____ the first woman homo erectus lived in Europe.

5. _____ the principles of the DNA clock

6. _____ Man and chimpanzees are more closely related than are man and gorilla

7. _____ the revolution of the earth around the sun

8. _____ Einstein's theory of gravitation

9. _____ the catastrophic mass extinction (of dinosaurs) in geologic time

10. _____ the evolution of dinosaurs into birds

New Vocabulary Revisited

Reinforce your familiarity with these words by writing in the one which fits the blank in the sentences below:

stereotype   incisive   to infer   inference   lexicon   orthodox
orthodoxy   phenomena   phenomenon   pluralistic   pluralism

1. Before the 1970s, belief in natural selection was _____ among British and American evolutionists.

2. Evolutionary biologists _____ the processes of change, although change cannot be observed.

3. Most scientific _____ in evolutionary biology cannot be observed.

4. Currently, we are in a period of _____ among evolutionary biologists as many theories are under investigation.

5. Newton, Einstein and Darwin were all _____ thinkers.

6. Each field of science has its own specialized terms, its own _____.

7. The idea that scientific experimentation in the controlled situation of a laboratory constitutes so-called scientific method is a _____.

TALKING/WRITING ABOUT ━━━━━━━━━━

1. From other subjects you have studied, with what theories in science are you familiar? Share your background knowledge with others in the group.

2. In the article, Gould presented a very strong case for the factual basis of evolution. In doing so, he was responding to discussions among non-scientists around the topic of "creationism."

   Use the *Reader's Guide to Periodical Literature* to find references for "creationism." With the materials you locate, write a report on the position of the creationists. Share your information with others in your group. Get feedback from them by circulating a first draft of your report for others to read and comment on.

Astronomers and Their Far-Out Plans

A Note About . . .

Isaac Asimov is one of the most prolific non-fiction writers. Trained as a scientist, he writes about every phase of it with zeal and enthusiasm. This selection is one of his short feature columns that appear in newspapers all over North America. Asimov also writes books and longer magazine articles.

BEFORE READING ━━━━━━━━━━━━━━━━

To Think About:

1. Read the title. *Far-out* has two meanings: a) a vast distance away—and so fits with "astronomers," or b) a popular expression for describing anything that is out-of-the-ordinary or unusual.

2. Read the first paragraph. Asimov knows that he must entice non-science readers into the material by firing their imaginations.

    Why does he write about "medieval cathedrals" in the first paragraph? How many years did it take, for example, to build the famous cathedral at Chartres, France? (An unabridged dictionary or encyclopedia will give the answer.) Do you know of any building project begun though not completed within your lifetime?

Vocabulary Preparation

Which of the words are unfamiliar? Which ones will you add to your Personal Vocabulary-Building Notebook?

on the brink
    a) brink—the edge of a steep place or of land bordering water
    b) metaphorically—at the moment before something begins
       • Which meaning does it have in paragraph 1?

probe
to probe
    a) in Asimov's context, a spaceship or whatever else will carry out the TAU Project in space
    b) use your English-English dictionary to find other meanings

jettisoned
    to throw out, to cast away (para. 6)

To Look For:

Look for the paragraphs that:

1. Capture the reader's imagination.
2. Explain the details of the TAU Project.
3. Justify the Project.
4. Reinforce the reader's enthusiasm and interest for it, though stating realistic problems.

Astronomers and Their Far-Out Plans

By Isaac Asimov

1   In modern science, we now stand on the brink of projects that, like medieval cathedrals, will be begun by those who will not witness the completion.

2   So far, for instance, we have sent probes to the outer planets. Voyager 2 has photographed Uranus and is heading out toward Neptune, the farthest known large planet, which it will reach in a couple of years. The project will have taken over a decade, but even middle-aged astronomers could expect to view the end.

3   Now, however, astronomers are speculating on the possibility of launching a probe that will be useful to us even when it is far beyond the outermost planet.

4   It would leave the Earth at a comparative low speed and will contain some 12½ tons of frozen xenon. This will be heated until its atoms break up into electrically charged fragments, ions. The ions will be expelled forcibly, little by little, so that the probe will slowly accelerate for a period of 10 years.

5   At the end of the 10-year acceleration, the xenon will be all gone, and by that time the probe will be moving at a speed of 225,000 miles per hour, or 62.5 miles per second. It will then be about 6 billion miles from Earth, well beyond the farthest point reached by that little, but far-out, planet, Pluto.

6   At that point the fuel tanks will be jettisoned and the probe itself, about 5½ tons in mass, will continue to move outward at a speed that will very slowly decrease because of the weak pull of the distant sun.

□

7   It will continue to drift outward for 40 more years until it is nearly 100 billion miles away from the sun. This is about a thousand times as far from the sun as we are. The distance of the Earth from the sun (93 million miles) is called an "astronomical unit," or "a.u." The distance of the probe after 50 years will be a thousand astronomical units, so it is called the "TAU project."

8   The TAU probe will have a large telescope on board and its job will be to send us pictures of the stars taken at increasingly large distances, until the final pictures are taken a thousand astronomical units away. After that, with the probe's energy supply gone, it will continue onward indefinitely and uselessly as earlier probes have.

9   Of what use will such distant pictures of stars be?

10   When stars are viewed from different places, the nearer ones seem to shift position compared to the farther ones. This shift is called *parallax*. The greater the shift, the nearer the star.

By measuring the size of the shift, we can calculate the distance of the star.

11   Unfortunately, even the nearest stars are so far away that the shift in position is exceedingly small. We can increase the shift by viewing the star from two places that are very distant from each other. On Earth, however, the farthest distance we can deal with is Earth's position in space at one time, and its position six months later when it is at the opposite end of its orbit. The extreme ends of the orbit are two astronomical units apart.

12   Such a difference in position enables us to measure the distance of stars up to values of about a hundred light-years. (A light-year is equal to 63,225 astronomical units.) These distances serve as a basis for the estimation of distance of still farther objects by somewhat less reliable methods.

13   The pictures of stars that the TAU probe will send us will show them at distances from us 500 times as great as the extreme width of Earth's orbit. By comparing the distant pictures with those we get from Earth, we will see much larger shifts of parallax and will be able to measure accurately the distances of objects as much as 1.5 million light-years away. Our knowledge of the dimensions of the universe will be enormously sharpened.

14   However, astronomers will have to wait 50 years after the probe is launched to get the final and best results. What's more, it is not likely that the launching can take place before the year 2000 because we must develop a reliable nuclear-powered engine that can heat and expel the xenon gas. In addition, we must also work out a laser communication system that will reach across the distance of a thousand astronomical units. Still, it's rather pleasant that astronomers are thinking of such "far-out" projects.

AFTER THE FIRST READING _____

Discuss your answers with a partner. Be ready to explain your answers to others in the group.

1.   What projects are astronomers on the brink of?

2.   How far out will the probe's journey go?

3.   Why won't the probe return to earth?

4.   If the probe is launched in the year 2000, when will astronomers begin to get results from it?

Read the selection again. Then, go on to the section Building Reading Skills.

BUILDING READING SKILLS ▬▬▬▬▬▬▬

Understanding Technical Terms

The writer doesn't expect readers to know technical terms from astronomy, so he tries to provide explanations for them in the context of the article. Guess the meaning of the following:

xenon   (para. 4, 5) "in ten years the xenon will be all gone"

          xenon is _____ a telescope

                    _____ a type of fuel

                    _____ a dessert

ions   (para. 4) "heated until atoms break up into . . ."

          ions are _____ an electrically charged atom

                    _____ a high-octane fuel

                    _____ a type of battery

parallax   (para. 10) "the greater the shift, the nearer the star"

          a parallax is _____ a shift in position of a star

                        _____ the two ends of earth's orbit

                        _____ a shift in position of one star in relation with

Making The Material Your Own

You are a non-scientist spokesperson helping the TAU Project seek funds to continue the work. You believe firmly in its goals. You are scheduled to address a group of concerned citizens who question the Project because of its cost.

Help yourself get ready to speak convincingly to them by writing summaries of the main ideas in the article. The outline below will help you to organize your talk on 3 × 5 notecards.

para.	*key phrase*	*purpose*
1–2	"on the brink"	to fire the audience's imagination
3–8	"Now, however"	The proposal: states how the TAU Project will work. (give specific details, for example, how astronomical units are calculated)

9	"of what use?"	States the question on everyone's mind: why do this?
10–13	"when . . ."	The justification: states the goals of the project (give specific details, for example, how are distances from stars measured?)
14	"However, "	The problems still to be solved: (give specific details:)

Use your summaries of the main ideas which you have put on 3 × 5 cards for an oral presentation. Practice with a partner.

TALKING/WRITING ABOUT ━━━━━━━━━

In your group, discuss these issues:

1. Have you ever visited a medieval cathedral, or some other old building?
    Tell the others:
    *   when was it constructed?
    *   by whom?
    *   for what purpose?
    *   what is the building's present condition?
    *   what efforts are being made to preserve it?

2. Are you in favor of spending public money on far-out space exploration? Or, do you believe projects close to home should receive support first? For example, education, low-cost housing, public transportation, cleaning up the environment?

3. What are problems with nuclear power? Are you in favor of developing more or less nuclear power as an energy source for the world's growing population?

Write about:

4. Manned/unmanned space probes: what are trade-offs? For example, the information provided to scientists, the liabilities, the benefits, the quality of information gathered, the knowledge and experience of living in space.

5. You are on the brink of taking a trip—into space. You've been assigned a place on a manned spaceship trip to _____. The trip is scheduled to take _____ years. What are your thoughts during the last minutes before leaving earth, or as you are preparing to leave?

Look back at Paul Theroux's writing (in Unit One) when he prepared for a walking trip around England for inspiration.

READING NON-FICTION BOOKS, REVIEWS, PROFILES

UNIT INTRODUCTION

READING NON-FICTION BOOKS, REVIEWS, PROFILES ━━━━━━━━━━━━━━━━━

The world of reading opens out to you in Unit Five. The possibilities for personal enrichment and enjoyment through reading are vast. Indeed, Unit Five selections present only a fragment of the possibilities. Non-fiction books (not a narrative or story, not-fiction) are written about every possible topic: history, biography, sports, music, art, science. Name your interest—there's a book for you.

The articles in Unit Five were selected to build on the idea that the more we know about a subject the more we enjoy reading about it. Therefore, you will find many of the ideas and personalities familiar from your reading in the other Units. In addition, three of the selections are related thematically to each other: You will read a review of a book written by a famous scientist, then an excerpt from a profile (a biographical sketch) about him, then some pages from the book itself.

By all means, after completing Unit Five, you should be ready to go out and select your own reading material.

Who Got Einstein's Office?

A Note About . . .

This selection is from a non-fiction book that is *not* altogether about Albert Einstein, but rather about the place where he had an office for the last 22 years of his life—the Institute for Advanced Studies in Princeton, New Jersey. It is the place where virtually all the personalities of 20th century physics and mathematics have worked at one time or another. Ed Regis, the author, wrote about their lives and achievements in *Who Got Einstein's Office?* To learn the answer to that question, you'll have to read the book.

BEFORE READING ━━━━━━━━━━━━━━

To Think About:

Read the title. Since Einstein has been the most familiar person in science during this century, his name alone attracts readers' attention.

The title implies:

- Einstein is no longer living.
- He was so important he must have occupied the best office at the Institute.
- The selection is informative, yet written with wit.

Vocabulary Preparation

These useful words are in the selection. Which ones will you add to your Personal Vocabulary-Building Notebook?

cult figure a famous person who has a vast following of admirers
ego (from psychology) a sense of self, "I"
hubris immense pride in self
humble modest, without pride
Platonic Heaven a heaven for people as great as the Greek philosopher Plato (the author's tongue-in-cheek expression; it sounds serious but the tone is light, he is playing with words)

To Look For:

1. What kind of person was Einstein?

2. What scientific questions were on Einstein's mind when he occupied the office at the Institute?

3. Einstein died in 1955. Do you think he used a computer in his work? Why did you select your answer?

Who Got Einstein's Office?

by Ed Regis

1 "You're writing a book on the Institute . . . so maybe you can tell me," says Rob Tubbs. Tubbs is one of the Institute's short-term members, a young mathematician specializing in transcendental number theory. We're leaving his office after an interview session, and he pulls the door closed and locks it.

2 "A lot of us have heard these rumors about how they left Einstein's office just as it was the day he died, that they haven't touched a thing. So, uh . . . is that really true, or what?"

3 Well, why not ask the question? It's the same thing everyone else assumes when they first come to the Institute. This is where Einstein was, for more than twenty years. . . . *Einstein*, the greatest scientist who ever lived. . . . *Einstein*, the one and only scientist whose name absolutely anyone can produce on short notice. Why wouldn't his office be preserved? . . . as even the man's very brain was, which is now floating in a jar of formaldehyde in the office of one Thomas Harvey, M.D., of Weston, Missouri. Surely they must have closed up Einstein's office, maybe sealed it off forever, like a time capsule, otherwise it would be . . . a profanation, a desecration, a sacrilege. Who could possibly work there? Who could fill his shoes? Who could sit in that same office, day in, day out, year after year, knowing that *here is where Albert Einstein did his thing?*

4 "Where is his office, anyway?" Rob Tubbs asks.

5 Albert Einstein was a world cult figure long before he came to the Institute for Advanced Study. When in 1919 astronomers confirmed his prediction that light rays would be bent by the sun's gravity, people went crazy. They named babies and cigars after him. The London Palladium offered him a three-week stand, asking him to name his own price. Two German professors made a "relativity film" and showed it on both sides of the Atlantic. When Einstein entered the home of J.B.S. Haldane to stay the night, Haldane's daughter took one look at the man and promptly fainted dead away. The press hailed Einstein's theories as the greatest achievement in the history of human thought, and Einstein himself as the greatest man who ever lived.

6 He was, after all, the messenger of the new order. Light has weight, space is warped, the universe has four dimensions. People loved it. They didn't know what any of it meant, of course, but that didn't matter.

Einstein did. He was the man who invented it all, who understood it. He became their hero, the new messiah, the First Knowledgian and Supreme Head of the Vast Physical Universe.

7   Einstein was revered as a god, but the man himself was the essence of modesty and kindliness, and he never understood why people made such a fuss. He, at least, treated others democratically, as equals: "I speak to everyone in the same way," he said, "whether he is the garbage man or the President of the University." Of course, if you were single-minded about it you could find some . . . exceptions, as for example the time he sent a paper to the *Physical Review*, and the editor dared to return it for revisions. *Well!* The poor editor had only done his job, sending Einstein's article—the same as he would anyone else's—to outside referees for evaluation. But this was not acceptable to Albert Einstein, who never sent one of his articles *there* again. But what does this prove? Only that the greatest physicist the world has ever known had, after all, an ego. If there's anything that most of the Institute's so-called prima donnas of science share, it's a healthy and well-developed ego.

8   In the world of ordinary men, Einstein may have been the humble genius who never wore socks (at least he wore shoes), but up there in the Platonic Heaven it was something else again. The man had this absolutely incredible hubris. He thought he might be able to understand the plan of the entire universe—the whole thing, from the largest galaxy to the smallest quark. He thought he could comprehend it all, that he could find a single overarching set of principles that would cover *everything*, in a theory of the unified field. And how would he do this but by theorizing, in the best Platonic-heavenly tradition. While the cyclotron people smashed their atoms to kingdom come, while the astronomers aimed their gigantic telescopes across billions of frigid light years, Einstein would close himself off in a room, pull the shades down, and, as he used to say, "I will a little think." He'd scribble out a few equations, make a few mental jottings, and lo and behold pretty soon he'd figure it all out. Just by thinking . . . no machines or instruments for him.

9   Someone once asked the great physicist where he kept his laboratory. Einstein smiled and took a fountain pen out of his pocket. "Here," he said.

AFTER READING ▬▬▬▬▬▬▬▬▬▬

Check all that are correct. According to the author, Einstein:

_____ was a cult figure   _____ didn't own a computer

_____ had hubris   _____ had a strong ego

_____ had humility   _____ probably had the best office in the building

Read the selection again. Then, go on to the section Building Reading Skills.

BUILDING READING SKILLS ▬▬▬▬▬▬▬

Understanding Paraphrase Expressions

The author uses words and phrases together which are very close in meaning, they are paraphrases of each other. If you know one, you can probably guess the others.

Check your English-English dictionary for the meaning of any one of the words in the groups below. Then guess the meaning of the others. Check your answers (guesses) in the dictionary. Compare your findings and answers with your partner.

1. para. 3   *meaning*

    profination   _____

    descretion   _____

    sacrilige   _____

2. para. 3

    who could possibly work there   _____

    who could fill his shoes   _____

    who could sit in the same office _____

3. para. 6

    hero   _____

    new messiah   _____

    First Knowledgian   _____

    Supreme Head of the Vast
       Physical Universe   _____

    Do you think the last two expressions are used tongue-in-cheek? Why?

Understanding Einstein

In the passage, the author tells his readers some of the characteristics of Albert Einstein. He presents a character sketch. Write your own character sketch by completing the sentences below. Write paraphrases; use the information in the article but express the ideas in your own words.

1. The world looked upon Albert Einstein as _____
    _____

2. But, he himself was _____
    _____
    _____

3. However, as a scientist he was _____
    _____

4. While he was _____,
    he was also _____
    _____

5. When the others worked in their labs or sat at their computers, Einstein
    _____
    _____

TALKING/WRITING ABOUT ━━━━━━━━━━

1. In a group, talk about the things one might find in Einstein's office . . . if it had been left untouched. Take notes during the brainstorming. Use the ideas that come out of the group's free discussion to write a feature story for your hometown newspaper.

    What I Was Surprised to Find in Einstein's Office
    by (your name)

2. If you had an opportunity to interview one of the following, who would you choose: Darwin, Einstein, Newton? Prepare for the interview by writing a list of questions to ask the famous scientist you have selected.

3. Or, would you prefer to interview one of the following writers: Isaac Asimov, Stephen Jay Gould, Paul Theroux, Ellen Goodman? Prepare for your interview by writing the questions you plan to ask during the interview.

4. With your partner, try out your interview questions: Your partner takes the role of the interviewee (the famous scientist or writer). Then exchange roles. Use the information to write a short feature story.

Reflections on Brains, Computers

A Note About . . .

Lee Dembart is a science writer, book reviewer, and reporter for a newspaper. In this book review, he indicates to his readers that he understands the questions which A-I (artificial intelligence) specialists are working on. He has done his homework thoroughly.

BEFORE READING

To Think About:

1. The title. This book review from a newspaper appears to have two titles:
   - What is the title of the book review? Who wrote the book review?

   - What is the name of the book which is reviewed?

   - Who wrote the book? _____

2. You have met Marvin Minsky before. He's one of the "science-fiction boys" interviewed by Kalbacker, the science writer. Scan Unit Four, Selection 2 to find his name and what he said.

3. Skim the first five or six paragraphs. Where is Minsky first mentioned? Why does the reviewer give four paragraphs of background information before mentioning the book?

Vocabulary Preparation

These are useful verbs to understand and use. Watch for them as you read. Which ones will you add to your Personal Vocabulary-Building Notebook?

allude to	to say indirectly
glean	to gather information
mimic	to copy or imitate
spur	to urge action

To Look For:

A good reviewer presents the highlights of the book, just enough to make you want to read it. How does Dembart accomplish this? Does he:

- use quotations?
- paraphrase the author's words?
- bring the reader into the author's context?

Reflections on Brains, Computers

By Lee Dembart

The Society of Mind by Marvin Minsky (Simon & Schuster: $18.95)

1   Language translation was an early goal of computer science, but not much is heard about it any more. The reason is simple: It doesn't work.

2   The reason it doesn't work says a lot about computers and languages and minds. It turns out that even if you have a comprehensive dictionary and a complete description of the grammars of both languages, translation cannot be done mechanically because the meaning of a sentence is not fully contained in its words.

3   There is something else, something extra, that a speaker and listener (or writer and reader) bring to language to fix its meaning. Without that something extra—context, if you will—the ambiguities of most words leave meanings unclear. Within the context, human speakers generally have little trouble figuring out what's being said. It's so easy that we don't think about

doing it. We hear other people talk and we immediately know what they mean, and that's that.

4   Computers are not nearly as clever. The question of how to give computers this kind of knowl-edge and how to give it to them in usable form has occupied the practitioners of artificial intelligence for some years now. It's not surprising that if you want to get machines to think like people, you should find out how people accomplish this trick.

5   And this, in turn, has led to theories of mind and how the brain works. Marvin Minsky of MIT, a pioneer in artificial intelligence and a man of wide and varied knowledge, has developed a theory, which he spins out in this book.

6   In Minsky's view, the mind is made up of agents directed to particular tasks, which oversee smaller subagents, which oversee smaller parts of the tasks at hand. Organization is the key to the whole enterprise. Hence the title, "The Society of

Mind." It's the constantly shifting organization of agents and subagents that gives the mind its versatility and depth.

7   Thus, a child's agent Play can turn on Play-With-Blocks (rather than Play-With-Dolls or Play-With-Animals), which in turn activates See, Grasp, Move and a host of other subagents who control various parts of the activity of building things with blocks. All the while, Play is holding off Sleep and Eat, which want to take control of the child's mind and get it to do something else.

8   Minsky shows how his theory accounts for learning and language and long- and short-term memory and perception and emotion and many other things we are familiar with as activities of mind. It's not clear whether his theory is a model, a useful analogy as it were, or whether he thinks the structures he proposes actually exist in the brain.

9   But he does make an intriguing argument,

which he supports with a bevy of fascinating examples while acknowledging that hardly anyone is very good at thinking about thinking and no one has any real sense of what's going on inside his head while he hatches ideas or talks to his neighbors or watches television or does anything else for that matter.

10   Some of the best parts of Minsky's book are the paradoxes he alludes to in thinking about thought. "Isn't it amazing that we can think, not knowing what it means to think?" Minsky asks. "Isn't it remarkable that we can get ideas, yet not explain what ideas are?" On the other hand, though, it's not so amazing that we can drive cars without knowing how an internal combustion engine works.

11   He is also aware that it is hard to think about the first principles of things because while these questions may be entertaining and engaging, they have never been answered, cannot now be answered and probably never will be answered. They recede into the dis-

tance forever. "I have specifically not asked for or proposed a definition of mind or consciousness or any such idea for exactly this reason. It doesn't get you very far. I assume that we all know what we mean when we refer to mind. It's the little voice inside your head."

12   Minsky's goal is to use whatever knowledge he can glean about the brain to help him build smarter computers. "We are still far from being able to create machines that do all the things people do," he acknowledges. "But this only means we need better theories about how thinking works."

13   Over the years, the pendulum has swung back and forth on this point. When they began this work, computer scientists thought the way to get computers to think was to have them mimic what the brain does. But this proved to be a very tough problem for the artificial intelligentsia for two reasons: One, they didn't know how to build such a machine, and two, they didn't know how the brain works in the first

place.

14   So the task shifted, and researchers said that computers did not have to function as brains do in order to carry out the same functions. After all, they said, cars don't move the way people walk, and airplanes don't fly the way birds do, so why should machines have to think the way people do? Humans have ways of accomplishing certain tasks, and machines have other ways of doing them.

15   But that hasn't worked either. Machines as machines have not been taught to think. So now they're back to trying to figure out how brains think, looking for a clue to how computers should do it.

16   In the end, this attention to the mind may turn out to be artificial intelligence's major contribution to knowledge. It has spurred theories of the mind and brain. But hard as it is to figure out how the brain works, it may be a snap compared to getting machines to do all of the things that brains do effortlessly and without thinking about them.

AFTER READING

Check all that are correct.

_____ The review contains quotations.

_____ The review contains paraphrases of the author's words-in-print.

_____ The review contains the reviewer's comments on the field of A-I.

Read the selection again. Then, go on to the section Building Reading Skills.

BUILDING READING SKILLS

Discovering the Organization

Find out how a skillful writer constructs a book review. Which paragraphs contain the following?

1. paragraphs _____
    Part I: Introduction. Gives information about the field of A-I. Captures reader's interest through discussion of language translation by computers.

2. paragraphs _____
    Part II: Minsky's ideas. Presents the heart of the book.

3. paragraphs _____
    Part III: Reviewer pulls the ideas together by synthesizing main points in the book with general information about A-I.

4. Which words link the ideas in Part I to Part II?

    _____

5. Which words link the ideas in Part II to Part III?

    _____

Quoting and Paraphrasing

In paragraphs 6–12, in places the reviewer uses direct quotation, in other places he paraphrases the author's words and ideas. Which of the verbal expressions listed below are used for these two purposes? Enter each one in the correct column.

in Minsky's view	(para 6)
Minsky shows	(para 8)
he does make . . . an argument	(para 9)
Minsky asks	(para 10)
he is also aware that	(para 11)
Minsky's goal is to use	(para 12)
he acknowledges	(para 12)

quoting   *paraphrasing*

Reinforcing Vocabulary

All the words listed below are in the review. Many have occurred in previous selections. Which ones have you entered into your Personal Vocabulary-Building Notebook? Which do you recognize? Which do you use? Test yourself by finding the context into which each fits. Compare your answers with your partner.

context   ambiguities   paradoxes   analogy   model   theory

1. Without that something extra— _____ if you will—the

    _____ of most words leave meanings unclear.

2. It's not clear whether his _____ is a _____ or a useful

    _____.

3. Some of the best parts of the book are the _____ he alludes to in thinking about thinking . . . "isn't it amazing we can think without knowing what it is to think?"

Contemplating Vocabulary

In paragraphs 2 and 3, the reviewer makes some observations about words and their meanings. Write a paraphrase of those comments. Add examples from your own experience with vocabulary learning. For example, how does context affect your learning of new words in English?

Share your completed paraphrase with your partner or with others in a small group.

TALKING/WRITING ABOUT ⎯⎯⎯⎯⎯⎯⎯⎯⎯

In your group, talk about these questions:

1. Did the reviewer like the book?
    - Is he enthusiastic about A-I?
    - Does he think the human brain works like a machine?
    - How can you tell what he believes?
    - Did he make any specific criticisms or comments about the book?
    - What are they?

2. Collect a few reviews of films, TV programs, or books. Reviews appear in newspapers, newsmagazines, along with other popular magazines and specialized journals. Bring them to class to share with the others. Are the reviewers you have selected critical? Do you agree with their criticism?

3. Are you ready to write a review? Make the assignment more interesting for yourself by selecting a book, film, or TV program about which you have considerable background knowledge. It may be a book about your own country or city, a film about a group of people or an activity you know well. Be critical but constructive. Get feedback from the others before you write a final draft.

Profile: Marvin Minsky

A Note About . . .

You've already met Jeremy Bernstein. He's the professor of physics who learned French while doing his post-graduate studies in Paris. Also a prolific author, he has written articles and profiles about his colleagues in science. This selection was taken from a much longer article about Marvin Minsky.

BEFORE READING

To Think About:

1. The title: A profile is a biographical study of a noteworthy individual, often quite lengthy. The form was developed by writers at *The New Yorker* magazine.
2. Read the first paragraph.
    *   For how long has Bernstein, the writer, known Minsky, the A-I scientist?
    *   How did they meet each other?
3. The selection consists of two sections: a brief sketch of Minsky and the writer's comments on A-I.

To Look For:

1. You will recognize the names of at least five scientific fields. What are they?
2. Why was Minsky attracted to A-I?
3. Who coined the term A-I?

Profile: Marvin Minsky

by Jeremy Bernstein

1   I have known Minsky for more than thirty years. When I first met him, in the late nineteen-forties, at Harvard, it was not entirely clear what his major academic field was—or, perhaps, what it wasn't. He was taking courses in musical composition with the composer Irving Fine. Although he was an undergraduate, he had his own laboratories—one in the psychology department and one in the biology department—and he was writing what turned out to be a brilliant and original senior mathematics thesis on a problem in topology.

2   For all his eclecticism, however, his basic interest seemed to be in the workings of the human mind. When he was a student, he has said, there appeared to him to be only three interesting problems in the world—or in the world of science, at least. "Genetics seemed to be pretty interesting, because nobody knew yet how it worked," he said. "But I wasn't sure that it was profound. The problems of physics seemed profound and solvable. It might have been nice to do physics. But the problem of intelligence seemed hopelessly profound. I can't remember considering anything else worth doing."

3   In later years, I had not been in touch with Minsky, but when I realized that something very new in the way of technology was engulfing us, I decided to look him up and ask him about it. I knew that he had been in the field of what is now called artificial intelligence, or A.I., even before it had a name. (The term "artificial intelligence" is usually attributed to John McCarthy, a former colleague of Minsky's at M.I.T. McCarthy, a mathematician and now a professor of computer science at Stanford, coined the phrase in the mid-nineteen-fifties to describe the ability of certain machines to do things that people are inclined to call intelligent. In 1958, McCarthy and Minsky created the Artificial Intelligence Group at M.I.T., and it soon became one of the most distinguished scientific enterprises in the world.)

4   During our talks, Minsky proved to be a fascinating conversationalist, with an engaging sense of humor and a luminous smile. He has one of the clearest minds I have ever encountered, and he is capable of elucidating the most complicated ideas in simple language—something that is possible only if one has a total mastery of the ideas.

5   One view of the goal of artificial intelligence would be to build a computer that, by its output, simply could not be distinguished from a mind. Since human minds play games like chess and checkers, do mathematics, write music, and read books, the ideal machine would have to be able to do all of these things at least as well as human beings do them. Obviously, to

make such a machine is an enormous task, perhaps an impossible one. People working in artificial intelligence, like any scientists confronted with an incredibly complex problem, have been trying to attack this task in pieces: thus the attempts to make machines—both the hardware and the necessary programs—that play games, that "understand" newspaper accounts, and that can recognize patterns.

6   That machines can already do all of these things with varying degrees of success is certainly a fact. The debate nowadays is over what this means. Are we thereby approaching a better understanding of the human mind? It is not entirely clear what would settle the debate. Even if a humanoid machine were built, many people would certainly argue that it did not really understand what it was doing, and that it was only simulating intelligence, while the real thing lay beyond it and would always lie beyond it. Minsky feels that there is at least a possibility that this might not be true. He sees the development of artificial intelligence as a kind of evolutionary process and thinks that just as intelligence developed in animals over a long sequence of trials and improvements, the same thing might happen in a shorter time as we guide the evolution of machines.

AFTER READING

1. Name five of the academic fields mentioned in the selection: _____

_____

2. Minsky was attracted to A-I because _____

_____

3. The term A-I was coined by _____

Read the selection again. Then, go on to the section Building Reading Skills.

BUILDING READING SKILLS ———————

Understanding Word Meanings from Context

If any of the following words were unfamiliar, you probably guessed them from the context as you read. You didn't take time to look them up in your dictionary. Put a check if the clues shown in the column below helped you. Write a brief definition of the word. Then consult the dictionary. Compare your findings with a partner.

1. para 2
   eclecticism   _____ he had . . . laboratories, in biology, in psychology

   ———————————————————————————————

2. para 2
   profound   _____ physics seemed profound and solvable but . . . intelligence seemed hopelessly profound

   ———————————————————————————————

3. para 3
   attributed   _____ the term A-I, coined by McCarthy, is attributed to him

   ———————————————————————————————

4. elucidating   _____ he elucidated the most complicated ideas in simple language

   ———————————————————————————————

5. para 6
   humanoid machine   _____ machines already do these things . . . a better understanding of the human mind

   ———————————————————————————————

6. para 6
   simulating   _____ the machine is not a human being, many would argue . . . the real thing lay behind it.

Turn now to Selection 4 on pages 200–203. Read the excerpts from *The Society of Mind* by Marvin Minsky. Be ready to talk and write about them.

The Society of Mind

by Marvin Minsky

Novelists and Reductionists

It's always best when mysteries can be explained in terms of things we know. But when we find this hard to do, we must decide whether to keep trying to make old theories work or to discard them and try new ones. I think this is partly a matter of personality. Let's call "Reductionists" those people who prefer to build on old ideas, and "Novelists" the ones who like to champion new hypotheses. Reductionists are usually right—at least at science's cautious core, where novelties rarely survive for long. Outside that realm, though, novelists reign, since older ideas have had more time to show their flaws.

It really is amazing how certain sciences depend upon so few kinds of explantions. The science of physics can now explain virtually everything we see, *at least in principle*, in terms of how a very few kinds of particles and force-fields interact. Over the past few centuries reductionism has been remarkably successful. What makes it possible to describe so much of the world in terms of so few basic rules? No one knows.

Many scientists look on chemistry and physics as ideal models of what psychology should be like. After all, the atoms in the brain are subject to the same all-inclusive physical laws that govern every other form of matter. Then can we also explain what our brains actually do entirely in terms of those same basic principles? The answer is no, simply because even if we understood how each of our billions of brain cells work separately, this would not tell us how the brain works as an agency. The "laws of thought" depend not only upon the properties of those brain cells, but also on how they are connected. And these connections are established not by the basic, "general" laws of physics, but by the particular arrangements of the millions of bits of information in our inherited genes. To be sure, "general" laws apply to everything. But, for that very reason, they can rarely explain anything in particular.

Does this mean that psychology must reject the laws of physics and find its own? Of course not. It is not a matter of *different* laws, but of *additional* kinds of theories and principles that operate at higher levels of organization. Our ideas of how *Builder* works as an agency need not, and must not, conflict with our knowledge of how *Builder*'s lower-level agents work. Each higher level of description must *add* to our knowledge about lower levels, rather than replace it. We'll return to the idea of "level" at many places in this book.

Will psychology ever resemble any of the sciences that have successfully reduced their subjects to only a very few principles? That depends on what you mean by "few." In physics, we're used to explanations in terms of perhaps a dozen basic principles. For psychology, our explanations will have to combine hundreds of smaller theories. To physicists, that number may seem too large. To humanists, it may seem too small.

Parts and Whole

We're often told that certain wholes are "more than the sum of their parts." We hear this expressed with reverent words like "holistic" and "gestalt," whose academic tones suggest that they refer to clear and definite ideas. But I suspect the actual function of such terms is to anesthetize a sense of ignorance. We say "gestalt" when things combine to act in ways we can't explain, "holistic" when we're caught off guard by unexpected happenings and realize we understand less than we thought we did. For example, consider the two sets of questions below, the first "subjective" and the second "objective":

What makes a drawing more than just its separate lines?
How is a personality more than a set of traits?
In what way is a culture more than a mere collection of customs?

What makes a tower more than separate blocks?
Why is a chain more than its various links?
How is a wall more than a set of many bricks?

Why do the "objective" questions seem less mysterious? Because we have good ways to answer them—in terms of how things interact. To explain how walls and towers work, we just point out how every block is held in place by its neighbors and by gravity. To explain why chainlinks cannot come apart, we can demonstrate how each would get in its neighbors' way. These explanations seem almost self-evident to adults. However, they did not seem so simple when we were children, and it took each of us several years to learn how real-world objects interact—for example, to prevent any two objects from ever being in the same place. We regard such knowledge as "obvious" only because we cannot remember how hard it was to learn.

Why does it seem so much harder to explain our reactions to drawings, personalities, and cultural traditions? Many people assume that those "subjective" kinds of questions are impossible to answer because they involve our minds. But that doesn't mean they can't be answered. It only means that we must first know more about our minds.

"Subjective" reactions are also based on how things interact. The difference is that here we are not concerned with objects in the world outside, but with processes inside our brains.

In other words, those questions about arts, traits, and styles of life are actually quite technical. They ask us to explain what happens among the agents in our minds. But this is a subject about which we have never learned very much—and neither have our sciences. Such questions will be answered in time. But it will just prolong the wait if we keep using pseudo-explanation words like "holistic" and "gestalt." True, sometimes giving names to things can help by leading us to focus on some mystery. It's harmful, though, when naming leads the mind to think that names alone bring meaning close.

——— Are People Machines? ———

Many people feel offended when their minds are likened to computer programs or machines. We've seen how a simple tower-building skill can be composed of smaller parts. But could anything like a real mind be made of stuff so trivial?

"Ridiculous," most people say. *"I certainly don't feel like a machine!"*

But if you're not a machine, what makes you an authority on what it feels like to be a machine? A person might reply, *"I think, therefore I know how the mind works."* But that would be suspiciously like saying, *"I drive my car, therefore I know how its engine works."* Knowing how to use something is not the same as knowing how it works.

"But everyone knows that machines can behave only in lifeless, mechanical ways."

This objection seems more reasonable: indeed, a person *ought* to feel offended at being likened to any *trivial* machine. But it seems to me that the word "machine" is getting to be out of date. For centuries, words like "mechanical" made us think of simple devices like pulleys, levers, locomotives, and typewriters. (the word "computerlike" inherited a similar sense of pettiness, of doing dull arithmetic by little steps.) But we ought to recognize that we're still in an early era of machines, with virtually no idea of what they may become. What if some visitor from Mars had come a billion years ago to judge the fate of earthly life from watching clumps of cells that hadn't even learned to crawl? In the same way, we cannot grasp the range of what machines may do in the future from seeing what's on view right now.

Our first intuitions about computers came from experiences with machines of the 1940s, which contained only thousands of parts. But a human brain contains billions of cells, each one complicated by itself and connected to many thousands of others. Present-day computers represent an intermediate degree of complexity; they now have millions of parts, and people already are building billion-part computers for research on Artificial Intelligence. And yet, in spite of what is happening, we continue to use old words as though there had been no change at all. We need to adapt our attitudes to phenomena that work on scales never before conceived. The term "machine" no longer takes us far enough.

But rhetoric won't settle anything. Let's put these arguments aside and try instead to understand what the vast, unknown mechanisms of the brain may do. Then we'll find more self-respect in knowing what wonderful machines we are.

TALKING/WRITING ABOUT ━━━━━━━━━━

After reading "Novelists and Reductionists," "Parts and Wholes" and "Are People Machines?": You should have the flavor of Minsky's writing, perhaps a taste for reading the entire book.

Work with a partner. Exchange information:

1. Scan back and pick out words and expressions which are familiar from reading other selections in *Reading by all Means*. For example: *theories, hypotheses*. What new words will you add to your Personal Vocabulary-Building Notebook?

2. Look back at Selection 4 in Unit Two, "Artificial Intelligence." Scan the material. How does it relate to Minsky's work?

3. How did the Review by Lee Dembart (Selection 2) prepare you to understand Minsky's writing? For example; What did Dembart say about Minsky's theory that the mind is made up of "agents?"

4.   In "Novelists and Reductionists:" (page 200)

In your own words, explain to your partner what "novelists" and "reductionists" are. Under which heading is physics? Under which is psychology? How would you classify other sciences, for example, biology? How do you think Minsky would classify genetics?

5.   What is the relationship between "builder" and "agency?"

6.   In "Parts and Wholes:" (page 201)

Explain to your partner what the difference in meaning is between the terms *subjective* and *objective*. Use Minsky's examples. Then add some from your own experience.

7.   In "Are People Machines?" (page 202)

Scan paragraphs 5, 6 of the "Profile" by Jeremy Bernstein:
  - What are the issues in the discussion about A-I and machines?
  - Are they technical issues, for example the complexity of building computers that simulate human intelligence; or, are they moral and ethical issues? For example: If such machines can be built, who will control their actions?
  - Do you think Minsky is positive about machines that can do humanoid tasks because he is a scientist who is challenged by difficult problems?
  - What are Minsky's ideas about evolution and machines that think like people?

8.   Collect some further reading materials on social-ethical issues and science. For example on issues of:

  - robotics: What happens in the workplace when machines replace people?
  - genetic engineering   What controls should be placed on developing lifeforms "in test-tubes?"

Prepare a report that presents both pro and con positions on the topic you choose. Share your drafts with others in the group who are working on a similar subject.

Credits

Pages 4–5, "Beyond Experience" edited by Donald Batchelder, Experiment Press, Brattleboro, Vermont; **pages 14–16**, "Learning French" from *The New Yorker*, February 2, 1987; **pages 20–26**, "You Have Left Your Lotus Pods on the Bus" copyright © 1977 by Paul Bowles. Reprinted from *The Collected Stories by Paul Bowles*, with the permission of Black Sparrow Press; **pages 31–32**, Reprinted from the *Saturday Evening Post* © 1960 Curtis Publishing Company; **pages 38–39**, J. Garrott Allen, M.D., *Los Angeles Times* Op-Ed 11/11/81; **pages 43–46**, from *Kingdom by the Sea* by Paul Theroux. Copyright © 1983 by Cape Cod Scriveners. Reprinted by permission of Houghton Mifflin Company; **pages 53–57**, from *Culture Learning: The Fifth Dimension in the Language Classroom* by Louise Damen, © 1987 Addison-Wesley Publishing Company, Inc.; **pages 61–63**, from *Biology* by John Kimball, Addison-Wesley Publishing Company; **pages 67–68**, from *Managing Organizational Behavior* by Philip Hunsacker and Curtis Cook, © 1986. Addison-Wesley Publishing Company; **pages 72–75**, from *Intelligence: The Eye, The Brain, and the Computer* by Martin Fischler and Oscar Firschein, © 1987, Addison-Wesley Publishing Company; **pages 79, 81, 83–86** from *Nuclear Almanac* by Philip Morrison and Jack Dennis, © 1984, Addison-Wesley Publishing Company, Reading, Massachusetts; **pages 93, 95–96**, Copyright © 1987 by The New York Times Company. Reprinted by permission; **pages 100–101**, © 1987, The Boston Globe Newspaper Company/Washington Post Writers Group. Reprinted with permission; **pages 106–107**, Copyright 1986, *Los Angeles Times*. Reprinted by permission; **pages 112–114**, S.B. Master is the President of Master-McNeil, Inc., an international naming consulting firm located in San Francisco; **pages 119–122**, *Breakthroughs!* co-authored by Dr. P. Ranganath Nayak and Dr. John M. Ketteringham with David Fishman as principal investigator, consultants with Arthur D. Little, Inc., International technology and management consulting firm; and Rawson Associates, publishers; **pages 127, 129**, by permission of AT&T © 1987; **pages 136–138**, Bettyann Kevles; **pages 141–144**, Warren Kalbacker; **pages 149–153**, Robert Ebisch; **pages 158–163**, Jared Diamond © 1984 Discover Publications; **pages 170–171**, Stephen Jay Gould © 1987 Discover Publications; **pages 176–177**, Isaac Asimov; **pages 185–186**, E. Regis, *Who Got Einstein's Office?* © 1987, Addison-Wesley Publishing Company, Reading, Massachusetts. Reprinted with permission; **pages 191–192**, Copyright 1987 *Los Angeles Times*. Reprinted by permission; **pages 197–198**, "Profile of Marvin Minsky" by Jeremy Bernstein, *The New Yorker* December 14, 1981; **pages 200–203**, Reprinted by permission of Simon and Schuster, Inc. All attempts have been made to reach the copyright holders of material in this book.

PHOTO CREDITS ────────────────────────

p. 13, Air France; p. 32, Ahsile Nibud; p. 79, U.S. Air Force Photo p. 101, Timex; p. 107, Bruce Anderson; p. 142, Zenith Radio Corporation; p. 175, Bild-Argenturen, National Aeronautics and Space Administration; p. 184, Smithsonian Institution.